T0205592

Fuzzy Management Methods

Series Editors

Andreas Meier, Fribourg, Switzerland

Witold Pedrycz, Edmonton, Canada

Edy Portmann, Bern, Switzerland

With today's information overload, it has become increasingly difficult to analyze the huge amounts of data and to generate appropriate management decisions. Furthermore, the data are often imprecise and will include both quantitative and qualitative elements. For these reasons it is important to extend traditional decision making processes by adding intuitive reasoning, human subjectivity and imprecision. To deal with uncertainty, vagueness, and imprecision, Lotfi A. Zadeh introduced fuzzy sets and fuzzy logic. In this book series "Fuzzy Management Methods" fuzzy logic is applied to extend portfolio analysis, scoring methods, customer relationship management, performance measurement, web reputation, web analytics and controlling, community marketing and other business domains to improve managerial decisions. Thus, fuzzy logic can be seen as a management method where appropriate concepts, software tools and languages build a powerful instrument for analyzing and controlling the business.

Jhonny Pincay Nieves

Smart Urban Logistics

Improving Delivery Services
by Computational Intelligence

 Springer

Jhonny Pincay Nieves
University of Fribourg
Fribourg, Switzerland

ISSN 2196-4130 ISSN 2196-4149 (electronic)
Fuzzy Management Methods
ISBN 978-3-031-16706-5 ISBN 978-3-031-16704-1 (eBook)
https://doi.org/10.1007/978-3-031-16704-1

This Springer imprint is published by the registered company Springer Nature Switzerland AG
The registered company address is: Gewerbestrasse 11, 6330 Cham, Switzerland

Este trabajo está dedicado a mi hermano Ian.
Me perdí gran parte de tu niñez, espero mi esfuerzo escribiendo este trabajo lo compense en algo.

Foreword

Around the globe, researchers and practitioners focus their work on improving living conditions in cities, that is, making cities smarter. It is a difficult task that encompasses optimization in an uncertain and dynamic environment. The concept Smart City is often focused on ensuring the efficiency in the optimization of traffic, public transport, distribution of resources, locations, and the like. This is a significant way of improving urban systems, however, simply put, not sufficient. We should go beyond that to cover citizens' needs.

Computational intelligence helps significantly in this direction. To be acceptable for all urban stakeholders' categories, solutions should be explainable and interpretable and should respect the citizens' privacy. This is a hard condition, which did not discourage Jhonny in his research endeavor. It was a challenge, which Jhonny solved marvelously.

The monograph focuses on the last-mile-delivery problem and proposes a new solution. The main problems are understanding traffic situations and reaching customers in their homes on the first try, keeping their privacy (location) non-disclosed. The model should cover traffic situations, explain them, predict them, and predict the citizens' behavior, whether they will be at the delivery place without tracing them. This task deals with imprecise data and unsharp rules. In this direction, a certain conception of interpretability and explainability is dealt with via fuzzy systems since they treat classes and concepts similarly to the human way of inference.

The monograph smoothly covers all considered aspects. Firstly, it elaborates on the topic, background, motivation, research questions, and research methods. The next part discusses the latest developments and definitions related to Smart Cities, smart mobility, and smart logistics of the last- mile delivery. The next part explains applied computational intelligence methods, namely fuzzy logic and the nature-inspired optimization, by swarm intelligence. The following part is devoted to managing and fuzzifying geospatial traffic data to extract relevant information, create a fuzzy rule- based system, and explain traffic information by the developed linguistic summarizations. The results are visualized on maps, which also contributes to legibility. The successive part is dedicated to the privacy-by-design requirement of public services, that is, how to classify the behavior of customers without disclosing an individual's location. For this task, traditional and fuzzy clustering and classification are developed. Next, the novel framework of fuzzy ant routing is proposed. The proposed framework is evaluated by simulation. The next part continues with the fuzzy and routing model. The evaluation of the prototype on the real data is developed and discussed in detail. Finally, the author answers the research questions and gives a critical reflection indicating benefits and weak points.

The monograph conveys a comprehensive view of the last-mile-delivery problem and merges approaches inspired by nature (fuzzy logic and ant colony optimization) with urban logistics. There is certainly a lot of work ahead. But this work paves the way for greater involvement of fuzzy approaches and ant colony optimization in these tasks and can inspire future research in the applicability of computational intelligence and especially explainability and interpretability for making cities smarter.

I am pleased to recommend this monograph to be used by communities of computational intelligence and Smart Cities.

VSB—Technical University of Ostrava   Miroslav Hudec
Ostrava, Czech Republic
July 2022

Preface

Mobility is crucial in the functioning of a city. Improving it is complex since it influences multiple aspects of a city. Nonetheless, any enhancement in mobility means that a wide range of citizens and economic sectors can profit from the potential benefits.

This work attempts to improve the service area of mobility, specifically, the last-mile delivery. To that end, a framework for improving the first-try success in the last-mile delivery is defined. In conceptualizing the framework, three artifacts were developed with a design science methodology and a transdisciplinary approach: an analysis tool for traffic areas addressing the uncertainty and incompleteness of geospatial data, a linguistic traffic summarizer, and a customer classifier that does not compromise their privacy. The author collaborated with two companies to design, implement, and evaluate the artifacts: *Swiss Post* and *Viasuisse AG*. The transdisciplinary collaboration enabled the artifacts to be developed incorporating the practical know-how of industrial practitioners while extending the scientific knowledge.

This book is split into five parts: The first part presents the motivation and objectives. The second part explores the theories in which this endeavor is grounded. Then, the third part is about building artifacts to address problems of traffic data analysis and ethical classification of postal customers. The fourth part introduces a conceptual framework built upon the outcome of the developed applications; an instantiation to evaluate the framework is also completed. The outcome, limitations, and conclusions are presented in the fifth part.

The outcome of the research works presented in this book demonstrates how complex processes and improvements can be performed using approximate methods that do not require large amounts of precise information while still achieving good results.

Fribourg, Switzerland Jhonny Pincay Nieves
July 2022

Acknowledgments

I would like to express my immense gratitude to Edy Portmann, who believed in me and supported me over the last few years. It was always great to pass by his office and get inspired by his ideas and vision for the world.

Especial thanks to Luis Terán for supporting all the projects I developed and opening me the doors of his house. It was great to have the warmth of an Ecuadorian home thousands of kilometers away from mine. I also thank Prof. Miroslav Hudec for his feedback and for contributing with his expertise to the improvement of this research effort.

Many thanks to my colleagues at the Human-IST Institute, especially to Moreno, Minh Tue, and José; without you guys, it would have been way harder. Thanks for the discussions, reviewing my book, the teamwork, and your friendship.

I would like to also thank the students that worked with me: Alvin Oti Mensah, Albana Jaha, Dardana Jaha, Hekuran Mulaki, and Jonas Diesbach. Your theses and seminar work were crucial to achieving the goals of this work.

The support of Viasuisse and the Swiss Post was also vital over the years. I thank the trust and openness that I received in the different meetings and workshops, especially from Damian Birch and Christoph Bürki.

Thanks to my chosen family in Ecuador (Pecadores) and in Germany (Boogies), even the shortest message reminded me that I always count on your support. A special shout out to Vanessa, Saúl, James, Paulina, Letty, Mónica, and Narcís. I am also thankful to the friends I made in Switzerland, especially to Jhon and Prisca. And of course, thank you so much to my beloved Andrea, Arielle, and Giovanni, without you, I probably would have given up. Thanks for always supporting me and encouraging me when I was feeling low.

Last but not least, my gratitude to my family. Many, many thanks for your support always, even across the distance, I could feel your love. Thank you, mami Betty, for always keeping things on track, so I didn't have to think about what was going on in Ecuador. You are my rock.

Working on this book was though work, even more during a global pandemic. There were times that it was almost impossible to concentrate with all the things happening. Thanks to all of you, I made it.

Contents

Part I Motivation and Objectives

1   Introduction 3
   1.1   Background and Motivation 3
   1.2   Research Objectives and Questions 5
   1.3   Methodology 6
      1.3.1   Design Science Research 6
      1.3.2   Transdisciplinary Research 8
   1.4   Outline 9
   1.5   Own Research Contribution 10
   References 13

Part II Theoretical Background

2   Insights into Smart Cities and Smart Logistics 17
   2.1   Smart Cities 17
      2.1.1   Cognitive and Human-Smart Cities 19
      2.1.2   Digital Ethics in Smart City Solutions 21
   2.2   Smart Mobility and Smart Logistics 23
      2.2.1   Current Research in Smart Logistics 24
      2.2.2   Trends and Challenges 26
   2.3   The Last-Mile Delivery 27
      2.3.1   Last-Mile Issues 27
      2.3.2   Last Mile at Swiss Post 28
   2.4   Final Remarks 29
   2.5   Further Readings 30
   References 30

3   Computational Intelligence 33
   3.1   Overview of Fuzzy Logic Approaches 33
      3.1.1   Fuzzy Sets Theory 33
      3.1.2   Linguistic Variables 38

       3.1.3   Linguistic Summaries 39
       3.1.4   Fuzzy Inference 40
       3.1.5   Design Criteria and Constraints for Fuzzy Systems 42
   3.2 Swarm Intelligence 45
       3.2.1   Basics of Swarm Intelligence 45
       3.2.2   Ant Colony Optimization 46
       3.2.3   Fuzzy Ant System Principles 49
       3.2.4   Trends and Challenges in Swarm Intelligence
               Applications 50
   3.3 Final Remarks 52
   3.4 Further Readings 52
   References 54

Part III   Applications

4 Fuzzifying Geospatial Traffic Data to Convey Information 59
   4.1 Critical Traffic Areas Identification 59
       4.1.1   Conceptual Development 59
       4.1.2   Type-2 Fuzzy Sets and Traffic Models 60
       4.1.3   Framework and Artifact Design 61
       4.1.4   Implementation and Results 67
       4.1.5   Summary and Lessons Learned 71
   4.2 Linguistic Summarization of Traffic Data 74
       4.2.1   Conceptual Development 74
       4.2.2   Linguistic Summaries for Traffic 75
       4.2.3   Framework and Artifact Design 76
       4.2.4   Implementation and Results 78
       4.2.5   Visualization of Results 81
       4.2.6   User's Evaluation 83
       4.2.7   Summary and Lessons Learned 84
   4.3 Final Remarks 85
   4.4 Further Readings 85
   References 86

5 Ethical Classification of Postal Customers 89
   5.1 Conceptual Development 89
   5.2 Modeling Customer's Characteristics 90
   5.3 Methodology 91
       5.3.1   Data Analysis 92
       5.3.2   K-means Clustering 92
       5.3.3   Fuzzy Clustering 93
       5.3.4   Fuzzy Inference 95
   5.4 Implementation and Results 96
       5.4.1   Customer Classification with K-means Clustering 98
       5.4.2   Customer Classification with Fuzzy Clustering 99
       5.4.3   Customer Classification with Fuzzy Inference 101

5.5   Analysis of Results 105
5.6   Conclusions and Lessons Learned 106
5.7   Further Readings 108
References 108

Part IV   Framework and Implementation

6   The Fuzzy Ant Routing (FAR) Conceptual Framework 113
6.1   Background 113
6.2   Outline of the Framework 114
6.3   Architecture and Component Interaction 115
    6.3.1   Data Layer 115
    6.3.2   Knowledge Layer 115
    6.3.3   Intelligence Layer 116
    6.3.4   Visualization Layer 118
6.4   Evaluation Design 118
    6.4.1   Validity in Simulation 120
    6.4.2   Simulation Setup 121
6.5   Further Readings 122
References 123

7   The FAR Artifact 125
7.1   Architecture and Introduction to the Artifact 125
    7.1.1   Data Sources Description 127
    7.1.2   Traffic Criticality 129
    7.1.3   Customer Delivery Success 130
    7.1.4   FAS Algorithm Implementation 131
    7.1.5   Web Interface 137
7.2   Evaluation 138
7.3   Analysis of Results and Lessons Learned 141
7.4   Further Readings 146
References 146

Part V   Conclusions

8   Outlook and Conclusions 151
8.1   Summary 151
8.2   Alignment with Research Questions and Discussion 152
8.3   Future Research 155
8.4   Outlook and Conclusions 156
References 158

**A   Data Structures of Probe Data of Delivery Vehicles and
Traffic Message Records Databases** 159

**B   Python Implementation of the Critical Traffic Areas
Identification Artifact** 161

**C Sample of Fuzzy Rules for the Customers' Presence at Home
   During the Mornings** 163

D Python Implementation of the FAS Algorithm 165

Acronyms 167

Glossary 169

List of Figures

Fig. 2.1   The Smart City Wheel by Cohen (2015) 18
Fig. 2.2   Framework for involving citizens in co-production
            process in Human-Smart Cities using collaborative events
            as proposed by Andreasyan et al. (2021) 20
Fig. 2.3   Digital ethics stack model as proposed by Terán et al.
            (2021) 23
Fig. 3.1   Fuzzy sets theory concepts and their relationships 34
Fig. 3.2   Examples of membership functions 36
Fig. 3.3   Triangular membership functions depicting a type-2
            fuzzy set as depicted in Pincay et al. (2021a) 37
Fig. 3.4   Example of terms of the linguistic variable $L = speed\ on$
            $a\ highway$ over the universe of discourse $X = [0, 120]$ 39
Fig. 3.5   Examples of ant behavior: (**a**) the ants follow a trail from
            their nest to a food source, (**b**) an obstacle forces them to
            find other routes, (**c**) some ants take one path, and others
            a different one, and (**d**) thanks for the strength of the
            pheromones the best path is discovered. Adapted from
            Teodorović (2008) 47
Fig. 3.6   Examples of how fuzzy methods can help to solve
            problems with incomplete data: (**a**) the distance of one
            path is unknown, and (**b**) the distance of the unknown
            path can be approximated to $long$ 53
Fig. 4.1   Framework to identify critical traffic areas based on
            type-2 fuzzy sets. Adapted from Pincay et al. (2021a) 62
Fig. 4.2   Example of the geohash hierarchical geospatial data
            structure at 3 levels. Adapted from Pincay et al. (2020a) 63
Fig. 4.3   The point $x = (46.8045, 7.169)$ mapped to geohash
            codes in levels 6 (left) and 7 (right). Adapted from Pincay
            et al. (2020a) 64
Fig. 4.4   Computations of the Fuzzy Inference Engine, adapted
            from Mendel (2007) 68

Fig. 4.5   IT2 FS for the variables ss (top) and tt (bottom). Adapted
            from Pincay et al. (2021a) 70
Fig. 4.6   Output type-2 fuzzy set depicting traffic criticality tc.
            Adapted from Pincay et al. (2021a) 71
Fig. 4.7   Sample output of the IT2 FLS for $ss = 0.45$ and
            $tt = 0.49$. The upper graphic denotes the type-2 result
            and the lower the type-reduced one. Adapted from Pincay
            et al. (2021a) 72
Fig. 4.8   Example of the visualization results from Pincay et al.
            (2021a) 73
Fig. 4.9   Method followed in the development of the LSs artifact.
            Adapted from Pincay et al. (2021b) 76
Fig. 4.10   Plot of the term sets for the quantifiers and summarizers
            of $DBLS_1$. Adapted from Pincay et al. (2021b) 79
Fig. 4.11   Plot of the term sets for summarizers of $DBLS_2$. Adapted
            from Pincay et al. (2021b) 80
Fig. 4.12   Example of the visualization results and linguistic
            summaries for the data of $DBLS_1$. The color of the
            circles depicts the total time of the traffic events and the
            size of the number of records on the specific location.
            Taken from Pincay et al. (2021b) 82
Fig. 4.13   Example of the visualization results and linguistic
            summaries for the data of $DBLS_2$. The orange color
            depicts areas with high traffic criticality, whereas the low
            traffic criticality areas are colored in green. Taken from
            Pincay et al. (2021b) 83
Fig. 5.1   Method followed in this study 91
Fig. 5.2   Distribution of successful and unsuccessful deliveries
            obtained from the studied dataset. Adapted from Jaha
            et al. (2021) 97
Fig. 5.3   PCA visualization of the customers in each of the clusters
            described in Table 5.1. Taken from Jaha et al. (2021) 99
Fig. 5.4   Evaluation of fuzzy partition coefficient (top), generalized
            silhouette (center), and fuzzy partition entropy (bottom)
            to identify and validate the number of clusters 100
Fig. 5.5   PCA visualization of the fuzzy clusters 102
Fig. 5.6   Fuzzy sets for the input variables of the inference for
            customer classification 103
Fig. 5.7   Fuzzy sets for the output of the inference for customer
            classification 103
Fig. 5.8   Membership network based on Fuzzy Logic 104
Fig. 5.9   SWOT analysis of the classification of customers
            performed with K-means, fuzzy clustering, and fuzzy
            inference 106
Fig. 6.1   FAR framework architecture 114

Fig. 6.2   Knowledge Layer process 116
Fig. 6.3   Example of membership functions of the fuzzy sets
            depicting traffic conditions 117
Fig. 6.4   Membership functions of the fuzzy sets depicting delivery
            success of parcels in a household 117
Fig. 6.5   Membership functions of the fuzzy sets depicting distance
            between locations (left) and pheromone intensity (right) 119
Fig. 7.1   Artifact usage in the formulation of the FAR artifact 126
Fig. 7.2   FAR artifact architecture 126
Fig. 7.3   Terms of the linguistic variable *traffic criticality* over the
            domain [0,1] 130
Fig. 7.4   Terms of the linguistic variable *delivery success* over the
            domain [0,1] 131
Fig. 7.5   Usage of geohashes to simplify the implementation of the
            FAS algorithm 132
Fig. 7.6   Terms of the linguistic variable *distance* over the domain
            [0,5] (top) and of the variable *pheromone intensity* over
            the domain [0,1] (bottom) 134
Fig. 7.7   Terms of the linguistic variable *utility* over the domain
            [0,1] 135
Fig. 7.8   Web interface of the FAR artifact 138
Fig. 7.9   Plot of results of the tour length for a number of customers
            for FAR and ACO (left) and of the execution times (right) 144
Fig. 7.10   SWOT analysis of FAR, ACO, and A* after the evaluation
            stage 145

List of Tables

Table 1.1   Design Science Research Guidelines and implementation
            in this research work. Adapted from Hevner et al. (2004)   7
Table 2.1   Results by ethical concerns and publication library as
            presented in Terán et al. (2021) 21
Table 4.1   Geohash precision levels and their respective bounding
            boxes (bbox) as presented in Pincay et al. (2020a) 64
Table 4.2   Sample of the fuzzy IF-THEN rules base of the IT2 FLS.
            Adapted from Pincay et al. (2021a) 71
Table 4.3   Validity values of LSs created from the linguistic term
            sets from the duration of all traffic incidents of $DBLS_1$.
            Adapted from Pincay et al. (2021b) 81
Table 5.1   K-means cluster characteristics. Adapted from Jaha et al.
            (2021) 98
Table 5.2   Top feature per daypart of each cluster. Adapted from
            Jaha et al. (2021) 98
Table 5.3   Fuzzy clusters characteristics 101
Table 5.4   Fuzzy cluster characteristics split into dayparts 101
Table 6.1   Parameters to be specified for the selection of the
            geographical area 122
Table 6.2   Parameters to be specified for the FAS algorithm and its
            ACO counterpart 122
Table 7.1   Sample of the records of the DS_1 used in the
            implementations of the FAR artifact 128
Table 7.2   Sample of the records of the DS_2 used in the
            implementations of the FAR artifact 129
Table 7.3   Sample of the records of the DS_1 and DS_2 merged on
            the geohash field 132
Table 7.4   Selection of fuzzy rules implemented for FAR artifact 135
Table 7.5   Parameters of FAS algorithm for the FAR prototype and
            its ACO counterpart 135

Table 7.6   Parameters of the selected geographical area for the
             evaluation of the FAR artifact 138
Table 7.7   Comparison of the results of the simulation to determine
             a delivery route for 5, 10, and 15 customers 140
Table 7.8   Comparison of the results of the simulation to determine
             a delivery route for 50 customers 142
Table A.1   Data structure of the probe data records ($DS_{1.1}$) used in
             the development of the FAR prototype 159
Table A.2   Data structure of the TMC records ($DS_{1.2}$) used in the
             development of the FAR prototype 160

List of Algorithms

3.1 ACO algorithm in pseudocode 48
3.2 FAS algorithm as proposed in Teodorović (2008) 50
6.1 FAS algorithm for the FAR theoretical framework in
    pseudocode 120

Part I
Motivation and Objectives

Chapter 1
Introduction

1.1 Background and Motivation

Smart Cities aim to enhance the city services to improve the quality of life and inclusion of people living or working there. Even though this concept has different connotations, one aspect all of them have in common is about the goal: they seek to enrich city functions using information technologies (Colombo et al., 2020a,b; Portmann et al., 2019). To achieve so, the participation of citizens, governments, and companies, as well as data availability, is vital.

There are different ways of benchmarking a Smart City. They are based on different indicators to depict their *smartness*. One well-establish method to benchmark them is the Smart City Wheel by Cohen (2015). The Smart City Wheel is a scoring model that uses six components: Smart Economy, Smart Government, Smart People, Smart Living, Smart Environment, and Smart Mobility. At the same time, each of the components has different categories.

From the components above, mobility is considered one of the most difficult to address given that it is directly related to environmental and economic aspects (Benevolo et al., 2016). Smart Mobility is intended to optimize the traffic flow and services that use the road and street networks. When the services are not related to public transportation (i.e., logistic and delivery services), then the concept of *Smart Logistics* is adopted (Korczak & Kijewska, 2019; Uckelmann, 2008).

Smart Logistics solutions are frequently built with traffic-related data. These data can exceptionally be difficult to examine and understand due to their heterogeneity and volume (Pincay et al., 2020b). Moreover, transportation and traffic parameters are defined in uncertain, imprecise, ambiguous, and subjective terms (Aftabuzzaman, 2007; Pincay et al., 2020). Furthermore, one key aspect that has to be considered when developing solutions is that citizens need to be informed. In the case of traffic matters, it can be difficult to communicate about it to an audience who not necessarily has technical knowledge.

© The Author(s), under exclusive license to Springer Nature Switzerland AG 2022
J. Pincay Nieves, *Smart Urban Logistics*, Fuzzy Management Methods,
https://doi.org/10.1007/978-3-031-16704-1_1

Research efforts in the field of advanced travel information systems and Smart Logistics have been directed toward determining where and when a traffic anomaly occurs and by how much travel time increases. Unmasking these mysteries could yield economic benefits in the form of less time spent on roads. This can be translated into more efficient services (i.e., delivery and transportation) and customer satisfaction.

Disregarding other constraints, reducing travel times means using less fuel and reducing vehicular pollutants, which directly affect the health of individuals. Furthermore, today most privately and publicly owned fleet vehicles are fitted with Global Positioning Systems (GPS), which allow their time-stamped positions, speed, and direction to be recorded. The data recorded by GPS and other embedded devices in vehicles designated to gather traffic information are known as floating car data. When the data is recorded by vehicles circulating to provide a service (e.g., taxis and logistic trucks), they are known as probe data.

Even though GPS devices record detailed information about a vehicle's position, they come with the disadvantages of losing local context, incompleteness, sparsity, and the complexities introduced as a consequence of business operations (Kwan, 2012; Seo et al., 2017). These are the main reasons why little to no attention is given to traffic data from logistics or delivery vehicles. For instance, road and speed restrictions, multiple delivery stops, and waiting on customers are some of the events recorded in delivery probe data that need to be handled appropriately when building travel time models.

Another issue is the low sample rate as logistic companies might have unique vehicles covering specific routes. Yet, it is also possible that this vehicle circulates through the same route every day, and thus, large amounts of data are produced. If the data collected by the logistic vehicles are adequately studied, important insights can be obtained, which could be used to draw insights from enterprise supply chains for strategic planning for example (Pang et al., 2013; Pincay et al., 2020).

To benefit from data of such nature, it is necessary to cope and deal with their uncertainty, incompleteness, and inaccuracy. Thus, this book proposes the usage of *Computational Intelligence (CI)* methods (Kramer, 2009) and *fuzzy set theory* (Zadeh et al., 1996) to address the difficulties of using probe and geospatial data. As a result, it will be possible to understand how traffic behaves on the roads and streets and to use that information to improve logistic services.

To that end, a conceptual framework designed upon theoretical and practical findings is proposed. This framework is later validated with one specific case of study. This case study entails the improvement of the first-attempt ratio for the last-mile delivery. In contrast to existing solutions, it is proposed to work only with data that do not compromise the customers' privacy (i.e., avoiding tracking data) and get insights about traffic without deploying many vehicles or expensive sensors. A solution like this is highly relevant since improving the way people move on the streets is crucial to shifting to smarter and more sustainable cities while respecting citizens' privacy.

Regarding the author's motivation to conduct this research work, the main one was applying the practical know-how of information technologies that he has acquired over the years with more advanced theories to create means that contribute to the well-being of people. Furthermore, the author considers that technology should empower human beings and not replace them. Thus, this research effort was conceived to help people perform their job more efficiently while also benefiting the receivers of those services.

Building bridges might be a more effective way of helping the transit, but since the author does not know how to do so, he decided to build bridges with data and computer science theories.

1.2 Research Objectives and Questions

This research effort proposes the application of CI methods firstly to understand how traffic behaves on the roads and streets and secondly to use that information to improve logistic services. One specific case of study is the improvement of the first-attempt ratio for the last-mile delivery using privacy-friendly data.

In the conceptual definitions and practical implementations, the following research questions are to be answered:

RQ1: What are the main factors that affect the last-mile delivery efficiency?

To answer this question, it is necessary first to understand the aspects that prevent customers from getting their parcels on the first-try delivery. A literature review study and workshops with people working in the logistics branch shall be conducted to this end.

The answers to this questioning are key to developing the methods that enable improving the efficiency of the last-mile delivery; such a capability potentially implies saving resources and thus reducing the consumption of energy and emission of pollutants since the tours of delivery fleets could be reduced (see Sect. 2.2).

RQ2: Which computational intelligence methods are suitable to obtain more efficient routes for the last-mile delivery?

Given the nature of the problem, computational intelligence methods could be used to improve delivery trucks' routing. However, all these methods and theories should be studied in detail to find viable ones. This question is important to answer given that not all existing methods might be suitable to handle uncertain and incomplete data. Through predefined criteria and a review of state of the art, it shall be possible to find an answer to these unknowns (see Chap. 3).

RQ3: How to get insights about critical traffic areas in cities that potentially impact delivery routes?

Provided that mostly all the last-mile delivery tasks take place using the streets, it is imperative to find ways to derive information of traffic anomalies on the delivery routes, given constraints such as incomplete data, limited available data (i.e., one single vehicle covering a certain route) and business operations (i.e., stops to perform the delivery of a parcel). Data aggregation utilizing granular methods and fuzzy analysis could be helpful to address these issues and derive information that allows identifying critical zones in the delivery routes. The evaluation of the findings can be performed through a prototype implementation and data simulations (see Chap. 4).

The potential findings are key to defining procedures that help using data that do not seem useful at first glance and unveiling non-evident information. Such procedures might not be only useful for traffic-related problems and might help to shed light on better ways of leveraging data in scenarios where data access is a constraint.

RQ4: How can postal customers be categorized without using explicit location data?

If customers can be categorized in terms of past deliveries, how can this categorization be? Moreover, how such information can be used toward reducing the failure delivery ratio. Fuzzy methods may be used to categorize the customers and avoid explicit location traces; data from past deliveries could be analyzed instead. Given the uncertainty that an analysis of such a nature entails, fuzzy methods could be applied, as the customer presence at home can be expressed in terms of membership functions (see Chap. 5).

Finding a solution to answer this interrogate is crucial to develop a privacy-friendly and ethical solution. Such a solution might be useful in other circumstances in which approximating the location of a person to provide a service is needed while respecting their privacy.

RQ5: How can we reduce the first-try delivery failure without compromising the customers' privacy?

With the findings from questions RQ1–RQ4, it should be possible to conceptualize and build a framework, which will provide the means to process information in a human-like way to enable handling imprecision derived from the nature of the problem and the data studied. The framework can be evaluated utilizing a prototype implementation and experiments (see Chaps. 6 and 7). Having a solution of this type might not only imply improving a service but also opens the door to the development of more human-centered solutions that could improve how people move on the streets. This aspect is important toward building better and smarter cities.

1.3 Methodology

This research effort was conducted following the guidelines of the Design Science Research (Hevner et al., 2004) and Transdisciplinary Research (Hadorn et al., 2008). The details are provided in the following sections.

1.3.1 Design Science Research

The guidelines of the design science for information systems methodology were followed because they enable the systematic implementation of artifacts to extend

Table 1.1 Design Science Research Guidelines and implementation in this research work. Adapted from Hevner et al. (2004)

Guideline	Description	Implementation
1st Design as an Artifact	Design science research must produce a viable artifact in the form of a construct, a model, a method, or an instantiation	The end goal is to implement an artifact that creates route plans to improve the first-try delivery for the last mile (see Chaps. 6 and 7)
2nd Problem Relevance	The objective of design science research is to develop technology-based solutions to important and relevant business problems	The methods to be used address the issue of working with imprecise and uncertain data (see Sect. 1.1 and Chap. 2)
3rd Design Evaluation	The utility, quality, and efficacy of a design artifact must be rigorously demonstrated via well-executed evaluation methods	Simulations are a suitable method to evaluate the intended artifact, and thus an evaluation method is designed grounded in them (see Chaps. 6 and 7)
4th Research Contributions	Effective design science research must provide clear and verifiable contributions in the areas of the design artifact, design foundations, and/or design methodologies	Several applications were implemented in the development of this project (see Chaps. 4 and 5)
5th Research Rigor	Design science research relies upon applying rigorous methods in both the construction and evaluation of the design artifact	The results and learning of the applications developed were published in peer-reviewed venues
6th Design as a Search Process	The search for an effective artifact requires utilizing available means to reach desired ends while satisfying laws in the problem environment	The end artifact was developed following a transdisciplinary approach, and industry practitioners were involved in the stages of development
7th Communication of Research	Design science research must be presented effectively both to technology-oriented and management-oriented audiences	Next to the results published, this book provides a comprehensive overview of the design and evaluation of the artifact (see Sect. 1.5)

existing knowledge while providing solutions to practical issues or organizational problems. This was a suitable method for this Ph.D. project as it was supported by industrial partners of the logistics and traffic management sectors.

The main output of the design science methodology is an *artifact*. Artifacts are defined as any material and organizational features that are socially recognized as bundles of hardware or software (e.g., algorithms, human–computer interfaces, methodologies, and design principles). Table 1.1 summarizes the guidelines of the design science research methodology and how they were implemented in this research work.

One of the outcomes of this book is the design and implementation of an application that enables creating routing plans for the last-mile delivery while addressing the challenges of visiting different locations under uncertain conditions and restrictions (1st guideline); thus, Chaps. 6 and 7 provide a comprehensive overview of the design and outcome of this book.

A solution as the one proposed could improve services in the domain of logistics and delivery without the need of using precise data sources, which is still a current problem (2nd guideline); hence, the problem statement and the motivation to address it are described in Sect. 1.1 and elaborated in Chap. 2. On the other hand, with the implementation of a prototype and through a designed evaluation method, it is possible to measure the utility and efficacy of the designed artifact (3rd guideline); therefore, the evaluation method used to assess the proposed solution is presented in Chaps. 6 and 7.

In the development of this research effort, several applications or artifacts were implemented and their results published (4th guideline). Such applications were conceived following rigorous research methods and properly evaluated (5th guideline). The specific process followed and the contributions done to the scientific community can be found in Chaps. 4 and 5.

Furthermore, this work was conducted following a transdisciplinary approach. With transdisciplinarity, it is meant that practitioners are involved in the development of the artifact, and not only findings from theoretical research but also practical experiences are incorporated in the process (Hadorn et al., 2008). Two industry partners of the postal service and traffic information management sectors participated actively in the development of this book, and thus, it enabled to development of an artifact that meets the desired ends (6th guideline).

Finally, the findings of the different development stages of this project were published (see Sect. 1.5), and with this book, a comprehensive overview of all of them is provided (7th guideline).

1.3.2 Transdisciplinary Research

As stated in the previous section, this research work was conducted in collaboration with industrial partners of the logistics and traffic management areas. The collaboration with such partners enabled to tackle the problems that this book addresses from a theoretical and a practical perspective. This means that the problems are solved with a transdisciplinary approach.

Transdisciplinary eases the process of collecting data and allows learning about the culture of the companies and how they incorporate their experience in the solution of the problems. This brings as an outcome that the solutions conceived indeed respond to practical needs while extending existing knowledge. Furthermore, a collaboration between academia and practice leads to collective knowledge and offers the opportunity of solving problems more efficiently and thus building a Collective Intelligence (D'Onofrio et al., 2019).

The author collaborated for nearly 2 years with the *Swiss Post*,[1] the national postal company of Switzerland, and completed an internship for 1 year in *Viasuisse AG*,[2] the competence center for traffic management information of Switzerland. This collaboration facilitated the development of the applications presented in Part III and the framework described in Part IV. Both parties acted as data and validation partners of the results of this project.

A transdisciplinary approach is a more holistic approach than the likes of classical research. Together with industrial partners, it is striven for a holistic picture in Smart City research (whole to parts). The ultimate goal is to create human-centered Smart Cities that enable looking at the problems from different angles by analyzing systems as a whole and then going by parts to find a solution.

1.4 Outline

This book is composed of five parts, with each part containing some chapters. The first and second parts introduce the thematic addressed in this work and the theoretical background in which the conception of the proposed solution is grounded. The third part presents artifacts or applications developed in the frame of the objectives of this project. The fourth part describes details about a conceptual framework to improve the last-mile delivery and its implementation. Finally, the fifth part closes the curtains with an alignment with the research questions and concluding remarks.

A brief description of the content of each chapter is presented next.

Part II: Theoretical Background
- *Chapter 2—Insights into Smart Cities and Smart Logistics.* This chapter reviews the current developments on the fields of Human-Smart Cities, Smart Logistics, digital ethics, as well as related work.
- *Chapter 3—Computational Intelligence.* The concepts of computational intelligence relevant to the conception of the framework and applications developed are described in this chapter. Special emphasis is given to the concept of swarm intelligence since it constitutes the angular stone in the development of this book.

Part III: Applications
- *Chapter 4—Fuzzifying Geospatial Traffic Data to Convey Information.* This chapter is dedicated to present the development process and outcome of an application that uses geospatial data and fuzzy methods to enable the analysis of traffic conditions.

---

[1] https://www.post.ch/de.

[2] https://viasuisse.ch/.

- *Chapter 5—Ethical Classification of Postal Customers.* This chapter outlines the methods followed in the development process and outcome of an application to classify customers of a postal service according to past deliveries while preserving their privacy.

Part IV: Framework and Implementation
- *Chapter 6—The Fuzzy Ant Routing (FAR) Conceptual Framework.* This chapter outlines the results of applying the concepts studied in Chap. 3 and the outcome of the applications developed in Chaps. 4 and 5 to conceptualize the FAR framework. This conceptual framework aims at creating routing plans for the last mile while addressing the challenges of visiting different locations under uncertain conditions and restrictions. Its components and architecture are described in detail. The design of the evaluation method to measure the utility of the framework is also presented.
- *Chapter 7—The FAR Artifact.* This chapter presents details of the implementation of one instantiation of the FAR conceptual framework. This artifact served as a proof of concept for the FAR framework. To demonstrate its utility, quality, and efficacy, the details about the evaluation process of the artifact are outlined.

Part V: Conclusions
- *Chapter 8—Outlook and Conclusions.* Concluding remarks, lessons learned, and future work are presented in this chapter.

1.5 Own Research Contribution

This section presents a list of the author's publications that were either presented at international conferences or submitted as book chapters in the frame of this work.

- *Pincay J., Portmann E., and Terán L. (2021b) Mining Linguistic Summaries in Traffic*: This case study article presents the details about the implementation of an artifact that uses traffic data databases to mine linguistic summaries. This work was conducted to determine ways in which fuzzy methods can help to convey information to non-technical people from complex data sources. The linguistic summaries are obtained and validated to ease the understanding of the data and to help users to convey information quickly and effectively. Through a web application that makes use of maps and accompanies them with the summaries, it was found that users with no experience in traffic analysis, do perceive that the mined linguistic summarizations helped them to understand data that would be rather complex, even through figures and statistical measures.
- *Pincay J., Portmann E., and Terán L. (2021a) Fuzzifying Geospatial Data to Identify Critical Traffic Areas*: This work describes how type-2 fuzzy sets can be used as a way of addressing incomplete geospatial information to create

a map for analysis of critical traffic areas. The development of this project enabled the usage of heterogeneous traffic data to analyze the traffic criticality of geographical areas, which was one of the main pillars in the formulation of the framework presented in Chap. 6. The end goal of this work was to define a procedure that enabled analyzing traffic aspects of roads and streets without the need of deploying a large number of sensors.

- *Jaha A., Jaha D., **Pincay J.**, Terán L., and Portmann, E. (2021) Privacy-Friendly Delivery Plan Recommender*: This paper describes the architecture of a recommender system targeted to providing dayparts recommendations of when parcel deliveries should take place to ensure a higher first-try delivery ratio. The results of this article provided important hints about the methods that can be used to classify customers without invading their privacy. Such results enable the formulation of the framework presented in Chap. 6.

- *Terán L., **Pincay J.**, Wallimann-Helmer I., and Portmann, E. (2021) A Literature Review on Digital Ethics from a Humanistic and Sustainable Perspective*: This work presents a literature review on digital ethics published from 2010 to 2020 in three technical libraries and one library maintained by the community of philosophers. The investigation process integrates a thorough review of digital ethics concepts in the leading academic libraries using keywords representing various concept applications. This theoretical research enabled the author to have a deeper understanding on how ethical aspects should be taken into account in the development of new solutions that use data from citizens.

- *Andreasyan N., Dorado A., Colombo M., Terán L., **Pincay J.**, Nguyen MT., and Portmann, E. (2021) Framework for Involving Citizens in Human Smart City Projects Using Collaborative Events*: This research proposes a framework to structure and facilitate collaboration between citizens and the public administration to solve problems linked to the city ecosystem, based on the concept and components of co-production. In this framework, the main point of contact between the public sector and citizens lies in different types of collaborative events and crowdsourcing campaigns. This article provided notions about how to approach experts and people in the development of solutions in a transdisciplinary environment.

- ***Pincay J.**, Portmann E., and Terán L. (2020b) Towards a Computational Intelligence Framework to Smartify the Last-Mile Delivery*: This article proposes a framework for the improvement of the first-try delivery by studying traffic on the streets and past delivery success as a way of approximating customers' presence at home. In contrast to existing solutions, it is proposed to work only with data that do not compromise the customers' privacy and to get insights about traffic features in cities without the need of deploying expensive equipment to obtain data. The feedback provided in the presentation and review of this research author helped to refine the framework presented in Chap. 6.

- ***Pincay J.**, Mensah A.O., Portmann E., and Terán L. (2020) Forecasting Travel Times with Space Partitioning Methods*: This research work proposes an approach to forecasting travel time through the use of probe data from logistic vehicles and simple mathematical models. The delivery operations of 5 months of a vehicle from the *Swiss Post*, the national postal service company of Switzerland, were studied in a segment-to-segment manner, following a four-step method. The execution of this project contributed to define the methods in the implementation of the project Fuzzifying Geospatial Data to Identify Critical Traffic Areas (Pincay et al., 2021a).

- **Pincay J., Mensah A.O., Portmann E., and Terán L.** *(2020a) Partitioning Space to Identify En-route Movement Patterns*: In this work, an approach is proposed for working with probe data toward discovering movement patterns in en-route operations of delivery vehicles. Given the spatio-temporal nature of the dataset used, geohash indexing was used to perform the data segmentation and analyze it at a coarse-to-fine granulation level. This effort helped defining a method to handle geospatial data and how to aggregate it to obtain insights. The outcome helped to define the method used in the development of the project Fuzzifying Geospatial Data to Identify Critical Traffic Areas (Pincay et al., 2021a).

Additionally, a list of articles that are not only directly related to this work but also played an essential role in the formation of the author of this book is also presented. All these publications lie in the area of Smart Cities.

- *Wallimann-Helmer I., Terán L., Portmann, E., Schübel H., and **Pincay J.** (2021) An Integrated Framework for Ethical and Sustainable Digitalization*: This paper develops the concept of an integrated framework to incorporate all relevant aspects of digital ethics by combining three categories of digital contexts: law and regulations, ethics and justice, and environmental sustainability.
- *Colombo M., **Pincay J.**, Lavrosky O., Iseli L., and Van Wezemael J. (2021) Streetwise: Mapping Citizens' Perceived Spatial Qualities*: In this work, Streetwise, the first map of the spatial quality of urban design of Switzerland, is presented. Crowdsourcing and neural networks are implemented in the development of this project.
- *Spring T., Ajro D., **Pincay J.**, Colombo M., and Portmann E. (2020) Jingle Jungle Maps-Capturing Urban Sounds and Emotions in Maps*: This paper presents the architecture of Jingle Jungle Maps, a tool for the visualization and localization of sounds in urban spaces. Through social media data gathered from Flickr, the researchers attempted to perform a text-based analysis on each post to identify noise sources and localize them on a map. To this end, computing with words and fuzzy logic methods were applied.
- *Colombo M., Nguyen M. T., and **Pincay J.** (2020b) Towards Human-Centered Smart City Solutions*: This tutorial had the objective of introducing the concept of Smart Cities and ways of making them smarter, especially from the perspective of citizens, and with a human-centered approach.
- *Terán, L., **Pincay J.**, Pacheco, D., Štěpnička, M., and Simancas-Racines (2020) Health Recommendation System Framework for the Optimization of Medical Decisions*: In this work, a theoretical framework for the design and implementation of the so-called project MedicGate, a smart social network to optimize medical decisions using cognitive computing, is presented.

- **Pincay J.**, *Terán L., and Portmann E. (2019) Health Recommender Systems: A State-of-the-Art Review*: This work provides insights about methods and techniques used in the design and development of health recommender systems, focusing on the areas or types of the recommendations these systems provide and the data representations they employ to build their knowledge base.

References

Aftabuzzaman, M. (2007). Measuring traffic congestion-a critical review. In *Proceedings of the 30th Australasian transport research forum* (pp. 1–16).

Andreasyan, N., Dorado, A. F. D., Colombo, M., Teran, L., Pincay, J., Nguyen, M. T., & Portmann, E. (2021). Framework for involving citizens in human smart city projects using collaborative events. In *Proceedings of the 2021 Eighth International Conference on eDemocracy eGovernment (ICEDEG)* (pp. 103–109).

Benevolo, C., Dameri, R. P. & D'auria, B. (2016). Smart mobility in smart city. In *Empowering organizations* (pp. 13–28). Springer.

Cohen, B. (2015). The smart city wheel. https://www.smart-circle.org/smartcity/blog/boyd-cohen-the-smart-city-wheel/, accessed: 2020-02-04.

Colombo, M., Hurle, S., Portmann, E., & Schäfer, E. (2020a). A framework for a crowdsourced creation of smart city wheels. In *Proceedings of the 2020 Seventh International Conference on eDemocracy and eGovernment (ICEDEG)* (pp. 305–308). IEEE.

Colombo, M., Nguyen, M. T. & Pincay, J. (2020b). Tutorial: Towards human-centered smart city solutions. In *Proceedings of the 2020 Seventh International Conference on eDemocracy and eGovernment (ICEDEG)* (pp. 3–5). IEEE.

Colombo, M., Pincay, J., Lavrovsky, O., Iseli, L., Van Wezemael, J., & Portmann, E. (2021). Streetwise: Mapping citizens' perceived spatial qualities. In *Proceedings of the 23rd International Conference on Enterprise Information Systems—Volume 1: ICEIS* (pp. 810–818). INSTICC, SciTePress.

D'Onofrio, S., Habenstein, A., & Portmann, E. (2019). Ontological design for cognitive cities: The new principle for future urban management. In *Driving the Development, Management, and Sustainability of Cognitive Cities* (pp. 183–211). IGI Global.

Hadorn, G. H., Biber-Klemm, S., Grossenbacher-Mansuy, W., Hoffmann-Riem, H., Joye, D., Pohl, C., Wiesmann, U., & Zemp, E. (2008). The emergence of transdisciplinarity as a form of research. In *Handbook of transdisciplinary research* (pp. 19–39). Springer.

Hevner, A. R., March, S. T., Park, J., & Ram, S. (2004). *Design science in information systems research* (pp. 75–105). JSTOR.

Jaha, A., Jaha, D., Pincay, J., Terán, L., & Portmann, E. (2021). Privacy-friendly delivery plan recommender. In *Proceedings of the 2021 Eighth International Conference on eDemocracy eGovernment (ICEDEG)* (pp. 146–151).

Korczak, J., & Kijewska, K. (2019). Smart logistics in the development of smart cities. *Transportation Research Procedia, 39*, 201–211.

Kramer, O. (2009). *Computational intelligence: Eine Einführung*. Springer.

Kwan, M. P. (2012). The uncertain geographic context problem. *Annals of the Association of American Geographers, 102*, 958–968.

Pang, L. X., Chawla, S., Liu, W., & Zheng, Y. (2013). On detection of emerging anomalous traffic patterns using gps data. *Data and Knowledge Engineering, 87*, 357–373.

Pincay, J., Terán, L., & Portmann, E. (2019). Health recommender systems: A state-of-the-art review. In *Proceedings of the 2019 Sixth International Conference on eDemocracy and eGovernment (ICEDEG)* (pp. 47–55). IEEE.

Pincay, J., Mensah, A., Portmann, E., & Terán, L. (2020). Forecasting travel times with space partitioning methods. In *Proceedings of the 6th International Conference on Geographical Information Systems Theory, Applications and Management—GISTAM* (pp. 151–159), INSTICC, SciTePress.

Pincay, J., Mensah, A. O., Portmann, E., & Terán, L. (2020a). Partitioning space to identify en-route movement patterns. In *Proceedings of the 2020 Seventh International Conference on eDemocracy and eGovernment (ICEDEG)* (pp. 43–49), IEEE.

Pincay, J., Portmann, E., & Terán, L. (2020b). Towards a computational intelligence framework to smartify the last-mile delivery. *POLIBITS, 62,* 85–91.

Pincay, J., Portmann, E., & Terán, L. (2021a). Fuzzifying geospatial data to identify critical traffic areas. In *Joint Proceedings of the 19th World Congress of the International Fuzzy Systems Association (IFSA), the 12th Conference of the European Society for Fuzzy Logic and Technology (EUSFLAT), and the 11th International Summer School on Aggregation Operators (AGOP)* (pp. 463–470). Atlantis Press.

Pincay, J., Portmann, E., & Terán, L. (2021b). Mining linguistic summaries in traffic. In *Proceedings of the 13th International Joint Conference on Computational Intelligence—FCTA* (pp. 169–176). INSTICC, SciTePress.

Portmann, E., Tabacchi, M. E., Seising, R., & Habenstein, A. (2019). *Designing cognitive cities.* Springer.

Seo, T., Bayen, A. M., Kusakabe, T., & Asakura, Y. (2017). Traffic state estimation on highway: A comprehensive survey. *Annual Reviews in Control, 43,* 128–151.

Spring, T., Ajro, D., Pincay, J., Colombo, M., & Portmann, E. (2020). Jingle jungle maps-capturing urban sounds and emotions in maps. In *Proceedings of the 2020 Seventh International Conference on eDemocracy and eGovernment (ICEDEG)* (pp. 36–42). IEEE.

Terán, L., Pincay, J., Pacheco, D., Štěpnička, M., & Simancas-Racines, D. (2020). Health recommendation system framework for the optimization of medical decisions. In *Cognitive Computing* (pp. 249–272). Springer.

Terán, L., Pincay, J., Wallimann-Helmer, I., & Portmann, E. (2021). A literature review on digital ethics from a humanistic and sustainable perspective. In *Proceedings of the 14th International Conference on Theory and Practice of Electronic Governance.* ICEGOV 2021, Association for Computing Machinery.

Uckelmann, D. (2008). A definition approach to smart logistics. In *Proceedings of the International Conference on Next Generation Wired/Wireless Networking* (pp. 273–284). Springer.

Wallimann-Helmer, I., Terán, L., Portmann, E., Schübel, H., & Pincay, J. (2021). An integrated framework for ethical and sustainable digitalization. In *Proceedings of the 2021 Eighth International Conference on eDemocracy eGovernment (ICEDEG)* (pp. 156–162).

Zadeh, L. A., Klir, G. J., & Yuan, B. (1996). *Fuzzy sets, fuzzy logic, and fuzzy systems: selected papers* (Vol. 6). World Scientific.

Part II
Theoretical Background

Chapter 2
Insights into Smart Cities and Smart Logistics

In this chapter, a review of the concepts mentioned above is presented in Sect. 2.1. Special emphasis is given to the research done so far in the field of logistics for cities or *Smart Logistics* in Sect. 2.2 and specifically for the problems of the last-mile delivery in Sect. 2.3) as these are the knowledge areas in which this work was conducted.

Furthermore, this chapter presents some of the results published in Andreasyan et al. (2021) and Terán et al. (2021), two projects in which the author participated. The results of these publications contributed to the enrichment of this book. The outcome of this review of concepts provided the basis to answer the *RQ1*.

2.1 Smart Cities

Defining the term *city* might result impossible since it is a multifaceted and complex phenomenon (Portmann et al., 2019). Many authors agree that cities can be described in terms of two dimensions: spatial-material and socio-cultural. From this perspective, cities could be characterized as settlements, with condensed infrastructure differentiated from non-urban areas, where large heterogeneous groups of people live and work (Mieg, 2013).

More than half of the global population lives in cities and megacities (cities with more than 10 million inhabitants). At first glance, this can be seen as a sign of progress and modernization. In a sense, it is, but it also brings challenges proper of having a large number of people living in a limited geographical area with limited infrastructure. Furthermore, issues such as environmental care, sustainable urban transportation, integration of people and cultures, and proper delivery of healthcare become more evident. Thus, one approach to address the problem of bringing well-being to the citizen is through the conception of *Smart Cities* (Meier & Portmann, 2017; Portmann et al., 2019).

© The Author(s), under exclusive license to Springer Nature Switzerland AG 2022
J. Pincay Nieves, *Smart Urban Logistics*, Fuzzy Management Methods,
https://doi.org/10.1007/978-3-031-16704-1_2

As for the definition of a city, the conceptualization of a Smart City has different shades. The common ground is, however, the enrichment of city functions through the use of information technologies with the goal of developing sustainable and citizen-friendly services (Colombo et al., 2020a). The collection and usage of city data is an important aspect that Smart Cities handle toward building more liveable and viable spaces (Portmann et al., 2019).

Different ways of measuring the smartness of a city exist. The Smart City Wheel by Cohen (2015) is one of the most well-established methods. The Smart City Wheel enables the scoring of a city to identify its strengths and weaknesses. It has six main components: Smart Economy, Smart Government, Smart People, Smart Living, Smart Environment, and Smart Mobility. Furthermore, each component is divided into three subcomponents. Smart City projects are generally implemented to meet a need in one of those subjects (Fig. 2.1).

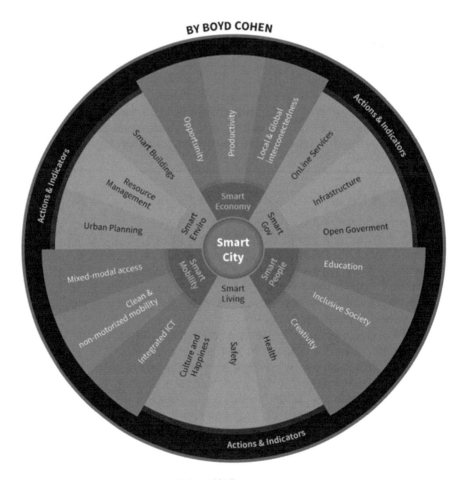

Fig. 2.1 The Smart City Wheel by Cohen (2015)

Nevertheless, how Smart Cities are being conceptualized and designed has raised some criticizing. The main concern is the excessive attention given to the technology involved in the development of solutions (Andreasyan et al., 2021). The technocentric view and top-down design of Smart Cities may imply that the needs of the citizens and people are not properly met, and thus, the goal of improving the way people live becomes far from being achieved.

On the one hand, services in the cities might be improved and become more efficient, but on the other hand they might not be answering the day-to-day citizen's needs. Thus, in recent years, the focus is shifting to designing cities with more active participation of the citizens to shape their places (Andreasyan et al., 2021; Dyer et al., 2017). Positioning the people's needs in the center of the design of any Smart City solution means that they could potentially be fully answered. However, the citizen needs to be included in all phases of the implementation of solutions, which is not always an easy task (Andreasyan et al., 2021).

With the involvement of citizens and by making them active actors in the conception of Smart City solutions, the traditional Smart City approach is conceptualized as *Cognitive City* and *Human-Smart City*. The following section elaborates on this matter.

2.1.1 Cognitive and Human-Smart Cities

Most of the Smart City initiatives have in common the collection, preparation, and analysis of data to get insights about the problems of a city and address them. Thus, a city could become smarter if all stakeholders living in it have access to high-quality data (Portmann et al., 2019).

The data collection process can be enhanced by involving all citizens and forming a network that enables collective intelligence: agents contributing with some level of intelligence to solve a problem as a collective in a better manner than individuals. Such agents need to be linked and in communication to be able to expand original knowledge (Portmann et al., 2019).

Humans are added to the loop in the Cognitive City approach, and communication between them is key to identifying problems and solving them. When the citizens are more than only in the loop, but in the center, then the approach is distinguished as *Human-Smart City*. Both concepts are nevertheless almost equivalent.

In both cases, the primary purpose is to actively involve citizens in shaping their city to meet their needs, wishes, and interests. Additionally, it is crucial to satisfy all stakeholders and balance eventual conflicts with the help of digital technology to form indeed a Human-Smart City (Andreasyan et al., 2021).

Nevertheless, involving people in the creation of a solution for the cities is not a straightforward task. Thus, diverse approaches exist to address this matter, such as designing city communication (Portmann et al., 2019), developing platforms to ease the communication of the citizens with the government (Tsampoulatidis et al.,

2013), and developing methods to establish a frame of techniques to involve people (Andreasyan et al., 2021).

To address the issue of involving citizens in Human-Smart City projects, a framework centered in the collaborative events (e.g., workshops, Makeathons, hackathons, and living labs) was introduced in Andreasyan et al. (2021). The goal of such a framework is to enable the identification of the role that citizens could have in the stages of the solution of the problems defined by any stakeholder of a city.

The framework considers contextual elements such as the definition of the problem, design constraints, and unexpected factors to implement a solution through the execution of collaborative events. Particular emphasis is given to the co-production stage of the solution. This stage encompasses fundamental steps in the conception solution for cities: co-commissioning, co-design, co-delivery, and co-assessment. All of them turn around the collaboration between the public or private sector and the citizens.

The framework also highlights the use of crowdsourcing () as a way of generating data from the population for problem solving. The advantage of using crowdsourcing is that a broader audience that is not necessarily specialized can be involved, especially when online means to collect data are used.

Figure 2.2 depicts the components of the framework to involve citizens in the development of Human-Smart City projects.

Furthermore, as per the results of an exploratory study conducted to evaluate the framework, it was found that the citizens are willing to collaborate with public and private institutions and invest time to promote solutions that indeed improve their well-being and the one of future generations.

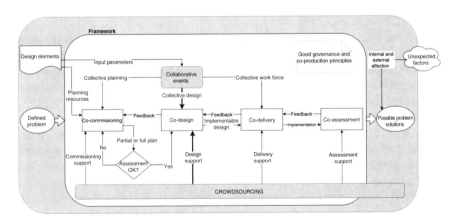

Fig. 2.2 Framework for involving citizens in co-production process in Human-Smart Cities using collaborative events as proposed by Andreasyan et al. (2021)

2.1.2 Digital Ethics in Smart City Solutions

Besides concerns of how to involve citizens in the development of Smart City solutions, there are other ones. Perhaps the most relevant is about how ethical the digital solutions being developed are.

The concept of digital ethics is not new. It is gaining more importance in the last decades as digital solutions are more and more integrated into the life of people in the form of smart services. As Painter et al. (2019) explain, for the success of any digital solution, it is vital to have ethically justified relationships among citizens and public and private sectors.

As per the results of the work conducted in Terán et al. (2021), Smart Cities are considered as services that are being studied in terms of how ethical the solutions implemented are. The delivery of Smart City services is considered as relevant as healthcare, government, and law ones, and thus, ethics remains a topic of concern. This study performed a systematic literature review of digital ethics publication in three technical libraries and one maintained by the community of philosophers from 2010 to 2020.

This endeavor also highlights the importance of several ethical challenges that the implementation of solutions should address: autonomy, discrimination, domination, exclusion, exploitation, inequality, justice, privacy, responsibility, trust, dignity, and truth. Privacy, responsibility, and trust are the ethical concerns that are mainly studied and thus put in evidence the moral matters that the designers of digital smart solutions should devote effort to. Table 2.1 summarizes the findings in regard to ethical concerns for the implementation of digital solutions by library explored.

Furthermore, a stack model for the development of a digital solution was also proposed. This model is founded on legal aspects and humanistic and sustainable

Table 2.1 Results by ethical concerns and publication library as presented in Terán et al. (2021)

Ethical concerns	IEEE Xplore	ACM	Springer link	PhilPapers
Autonomy	31	32	17	25
Discrimination	14	24	10	21
Domination			2	2
Exclusion	5	11	9	9
Exploitation	8	12	6	4
Inequality	8	14	9	8
Justice	23	14	19	28
Privacy	52	34	27	38
Responsibility	43	44	29	37
Trust	46	61	19	30
Dignity	10	12	9	13
Truth	12	19	11	16
Total	252	277	167	231

values to enable the implementation of products or platforms that meet citizens' needs while respecting ethical aspects. Its main components are as follows:

2.1.2.1   Legal Perspective

• **Legal Framework:** Any data-based project has to have its foundation on data privacy and its legal implications. One example of this is the legal framework of the European Union.

2.1.2.2   IT Perspective

• **Data Principles:** The second layer of the model describes the different digital principles based on legal frameworks. An example of this layer could be the General Data Protection Regulation (GDPR)[1] applied in the European Union; it includes several principles required to provide digital services.
• **Humanistic and Sustainable Principles:** The third layer of the stack model includes humanistic ethical and sustainable principles. This set of principles' objective is to guarantee that the services provided to citizens/customers comply with an ethical framework that respects nature and social boundaries.
• **Technology Enablers:** The fourth layer of the stack model focuses on the different technological enablers (e.g., interactive machine learning, security, human-centered systems, explainable artificial intelligence, federated learning, privacy by design, blockchain), ethical and sustainable services to citizens/customers. The development of technological enablers must comply with the data, humanistic, and sustainable principles.
• **Services:** The fifth layer reflects on citizens and companies (e.g., smart voting, Smart Cities, smart gov, smart health, business intelligence, smart logistics). This layer is significantly improved and better formulated by all previous layers of the stack model.

2.1.2.3   Citizen Perspective

• **Citizen and Customer Issues/needs:** The sixth layer reflects on citizen and customer issues and needs. The long arrow of digital transformation points to the upper layers starting from citizen and customer needs. Customer needs cannot be met and identified if the service provider does not place and develop all previous layers.

---

[1] https://gdpr.eu.

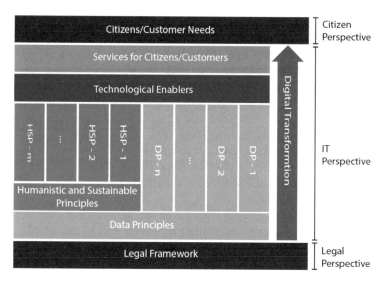

Fig. 2.3 Digital ethics stack model as proposed by Terán et al. (2021)

Figure 2.3 depicts the ethical stack model. As it can be observed, data values and humanistic and sustainable principles are located at the core and thus are the angular stones when attempting to build ethical and smart solutions.

The implementation of this book was performed following the frame provided by this stack model, having at the core respecting the privacy of the customers and using more bio-inspired models that potentially enable saving energy (compared to the likes of machine learning-based implementations).

2.2 Smart Mobility and Smart Logistics

As proposed by Cohen (2015), among the components of the Smart City Wheel, there is *Smart Mobility*. Mobility is key in the functioning of a city, it influences many aspects of life in the city such as traffic, pollution, high transportation costs, and logistics (Benevolo et al., 2016), and thus, mobility is one of the most complex topics to address when it comes to improvement or *smartify*.

Some authors see Smart Mobility as the improvement of transportation with information technologies (following the technocentric view of Smart Cities). Its most important objectives, according to Benevolo et al. (2016), are:

- Reducing pollution
- Reducing traffic congestion
- Increasing people safety
- Reducing noise pollution
- Improving transfer speed and transfer costs

Smartifying mobility is thus a complex topic to address since it intersects the interests of different stakeholders in a city (i.e., citizens, municipality, transport providers, and logistic companies). This, however, also implies that when Smart Mobility solutions are implemented, they could benefit the whole community.

One of the areas of Smart Logistics characterized by a high intensity of development with information technologies is the logistics sector (i.e., transportation of goods). Smart Logistics deals with the efficient planning and scheduling of services that use the roads for their operations (Jabeur et al., 2017). Typically, Smart Logistic solutions use traffic-related and probe data that most of the time come incomplete, and it is challenging to convey information from (Pincay et al., 2020a). Additionally, many existing tools are not able to handle the quantity and quality of the information available (Van Woensel, 2012).

When correctly handled, traffic-related data can help to predict the occurrence of problems on the roads and find possible solutions. This translates into possible economic benefits for logistic companies, better customers' services, and improved circulation on the transportation networks for the companies and the people. Thus, there is the need to use more approximate methods that enable handling the inaccuracy and incompleteness and still perform inferences or make decisions with significant good results.

In the following sections, more details about current research topics in Smart Logistics are presented to frame the target and scope of this book.

2.2.1   Current Research in Smart Logistics

Research in Smart Logistics ranges from projects targeted to optimize routes for transportation companies to city-wide projects to improve transit and public transportation.

Traditionally, the research in Smart Logistics has been focusing on having the right products at the right place and time (Uckelmann, 2008). Until a certain point, this was possible to achieve following mathematical models that predicted how traffic was going to behave over a year, for example. However, the dynamics on streets and roads have changed drastically mainly because of the increase of urban populations and consumption habits. Thus, research on Smart Logistics has been focusing on addressing those dynamic changes using new methods and technologies still to fulfill the requirements of service providers and citizens.

The authors Papoutsis and Nathanail (2016) attempted to categorize the areas of research of the Smart Logistic in the following:

- *Logistic models for the private sector:* Investigation in this field focuses primarily on improving delivery times and optimizing the supply chains networks of companies.
- *Capacity sharing*: Research in this area is targeted to enhance the way infrastructure and equipment are shared among logistic suppliers.

- *Infrastructure development and design of networks*: Developments in this field deal with the design of road networks and supply chains considering the dynamic changes in traffic.
- *Intelligence transport systems*: One of the most explored areas that study the inclusion of information technologies to improve traffic and transportation systems.
- *Green logistics*: Research conducted in this field studies the usage of methods to produce the most negligible impact possible when designing transportation models.
- *Routing optimization and vehicle routing*: A prominent research field of Smart Logistics that aims at finding the best routes for the delivery of services that use the roads and streets.

From the list above, the topics of logistic models and routing optimization are the ones that are being widely studied since they have several challenges to address. One of them is to deal with the amount of inaccurate data generated. Most projects are being developed with GPS-based data that result at times challenging to process given their point-to-point recording and their variability. For instance, if traffic is to be studied with floating car data of logistic trucks, it has to be addressed and considered that the truck might stop because of the business model (i.e., to deliver parcels). Thus, if a vehicle stops in this case, it does not mean it is stacked in traffic.

However, when processed with appropriate methods, such data can be used to get insights about what is happening on the road and street networks to optimize routes.

Mainly speaking of routing problems, floating car data are being used to create new plans that seek to optimize resources and reduce travel times (e.g., Pincay et al. 2020; Wang et al. 2014; Zhang et al. 2017) while avoiding invading the privacy of the people (i.e., constant tracking of location).

In accordance with Mańdziuk (2018), the mainstream of Vehicle Routing Problem (VRP) research is being developed in three axes:

1. Current demands of societal changes, including green logistics, ad hoc delivery, and last-mile delivery
2. Combination of vehicle routing aspects with practical-motivated issues, for example, vehicle routing with backhauls and rich vehicle routing
3. New formulations targeted at satisfying demands of specific sectors such as the transportation of dangerous materials or the humanitarian transportation post-disasters

In the following section, more details about the trends and challenges of the research in Smart Logistics are presented.

2.2.2 *Trends and Challenges*

The mainstream of Smart Logistics research is directed to the conception of intelligent logistics. An important aspect is that these solutions have to be accepted by the economic and social actors, given that transportation influences these sectors considerably.

In terms of scientific production, as reported by Mańdziuk (2018), there has been a considerable increase in the number of publications in the last decades. From 2000 to 2012, 19 papers were published (in selected journals), whereas 83 publications were found between 2013 and 2017. This evidences a rising interest in smartifying the way people are moving on the roads.

Specifically for the field of VRP, the new topics that are being studied are last-mile delivery, crowdshipping, green vehicle routing, and autonomous delivery vehicle (Mańdziuk, 2018). From them, the topics with more publications from 2000 are green vehicle routing (67 publications), and less attention is given to last-mile delivery problems (25 publications) and autonomous delivery vehicles (21 publications).

Regarding the methods used in the development of the solutions, they include Monte Carlo simulations, graph theory, bi-level optimization, hyper-heuristics, and CI methods (Korczak & Kijewska, 2019; Mańdziuk, 2018).

In the early stages of research in the logistics field, the mainly used approaches were exact methods (e.g., branch and bound or branch and cut). However, weaknesses of such methods included the need for exact data to perform optimizations. Obtaining exact data has become more complicated given new laws turning around ethics and privacy; this motivated a shift to implement solutions based on more approximate methods that still enable achieving the goals while requiring fewer amounts of data.

One of the approaches that has attracted interest from the scientific community in the last years is the application of cognitive-motivated methods, which are based on bio-inspired models and the way humans think to solve problems. The idea is to include humans in the development of solutions and that they can solve problems in collaboration with machines. Humans can participate in adjusting parameters when creating better routes, for example, or using their knowledge to validate and implement systems.

However, involving humans in -the loop in the development of Smart Logistics solutions is still a hard task. The main reason for this is that traffic information can be difficult to understand for non-specialized people. Additionally, the knowledge that they could contribute can be challenging to represent. Thus, current efforts are addressed to find ways of improving the exchange of information between broader audiences in traffic- and transportation-related methods. Implementing methods to represent and use the knowledge of people who use the roads and streets is also of interest since their experience can enrich and improve the quality of the results obtained by Smart Logistics solutions.

2.3 The Last-Mile Delivery

In terms of logistic services, the last mile depicts the process of delivering a parcel from a local delivery point to the doorstep of the customers; it is basically the last stage of a long chain to provide delivery service to a customer. The last-mile delivery is one of the most challenging logistics problems (Seghezzi et al., 2021) since it takes place in a dynamic environment (i.e., streets with traffic). Also, it might not be as efficient as the other stages of the supply chain, as the simple fact that a customer is not at home at the delivery time affects the overall service. As it was presented in the previous section, research in the area of last-mile delivery has been increasing, but it has not been as explored as other Smart Logistics-related topics.

In the following sections, the current problems that need to be addressed to improve the last-mile delivery and the solution approach in this regard for *Swiss Post*, one of the partner companies that supported this project, are presented.

2.3.1 Last-Mile Issues

According to Mangiaracina et al. (2019), the challenges of the last-mile delivery can be analyzed from three perspectives: environmental sustainability, effectiveness, and cost efficiency. However, all of them turn around the effectiveness since improving the first-try delivery ratio saves resources and reduces the number of trips (which translates into less fuel consumption, for example).

The effectiveness can be addressed from two perspectives: improving the traditional delivery model and finding more innovative solutions. With the first perspective, it is dealt with the routing of vehicles to find better routes, and with the second, the introduction of novel elements (i.e., autonomous vehicles and drones) is studied (Mangiaracina et al., 2019).

Even though the delivery using autonomous vehicles seems promising, they are still far from being mature, and there are many implications that need to be addressed. In the meantime, the traditional model has to be still improved and enhanced.

The solutions aiming to improve the last-mile delivery in the traditional model can be grouped into four categories (Van Duin et al., 2016):

- *Change in location*: Leaving parcels at an alternative location
- *Change in time*: Delivering parcels at the times indicated by the customer
- *Change in route*: Closely related to changes in time, meaning that the route is adapted according to the time availability of the customers
- *Change in behavior*: Triggering customers to choose certain characteristics or delivery time by offering cheaper fares, for example

Despite all of these possible solutions, customers still prefer the delivery at home (Mangiaracina et al., 2019; Van Duin et al., 2016). Thus, efforts are targeted toward finding the best times to deliver a parcel to increase the first-try delivery ratio considering aspects such as traffic when creating new and more efficient delivery tours.

While most of the solutions found in the literature claim to have improved the efficiency of the last-mile delivery, most of them face challenges when it comes to obtaining the necessary data to develop prediction models. Logistic and delivery companies frequently own floating car data of their trucks. On the one hand, that is a valuable source to obtain insights into what is happening on the roads. On the other hand, these data often come incomplete and are complex as a consequence of business operations (e.g., road and speed restrictions, multiple delivery stops, and waiting on customers) (Mańdziuk, 2018; Van Duin et al., 2016).

Furthermore, it is difficult to accurately predict where and when a customer is going to be at a particular moment (Mangiaracina et al., 2019; Pan et al., 2017). Many approaches aim at tracking the location of the customer, but given that privacy is a current primary concern, most of the time, customers are not willing to share their location with companies. Besides, some laws need to be accomplished (e.g., General Data Protection Regulation—GDPR), resulting in an even more complex problem.

Thus, research to improve the last-mile delivery has to address those problems to implement more appropriate solutions.

2.3.2 Last Mile at Swiss Post

The *Swiss Post*, the largest postal delivery provider of Switzerland, also faces some of the typical problems of the last-mile delivery.

The number of parcels transported by *Swiss Post* in 2015 was 115 million (+ 3% compared to 2014). Consumers are increasingly buying in online shops and have the goods delivered by *Swiss Post*, and there are no signs of them slowing down. However, there is often no one at home to receive parcels in person during the day. Even neighbors, with whom shipments could be deposited earlier, are often no longer available since they are on the move themselves. At the same time, private individuals give parcels very regularly, for example, with items that they sell on auction platforms or returns of goods purchased online. These customers often cannot or do not want to be forced to go to the opening times of the classic of a postal office. Everyone expects a "now and everywhere" type of service from modern logistics. Fixed addresses and fixed opening times at a specific location are increasingly viewed as outmoded concepts of the past. People require solutions that are better to the new (individualized) lifestyle and rhythm of the present (Pletscher et al., 2016).

To address those problems, the *Swiss Post* has implemented a corporate strategy with a focus on improving its services with the application of information technologies. This strategy also implied creating alliances with universities of Switzerland to foster research projects that help to solve these issues. The author of this book was one of the Ph.D. students who collaborated in researching new solutions for them.

As part of the transdisciplinary research in which this effort was conducted, the author participated in September of 2018 in a Makeathon,[2] an event in which people devise solutions on a topic organized by *Swiss Post* to conceptualize solutions for the last mile. This event allowed the author to become aware of the specific problems that the company is facing. Subsequent workshops and discussions with representatives of *Swiss Post* allowed identifying the main problems that this research approach addresses:

1. Availability of floating car data with information about the location and states of the delivery vehicles in operation hours. However, these data are not leveraged to obtain any analytic that can help approximate traffic events.
2. Availability of all the history of deliveries to customers but given privacy issues and lack of more precise data is not possible to create customer profiles about the presence of customers at home. Such a capability could enable the improvement of the delivery routes.
3. The number of failed deliveries is still high, and most of the time, the customer has to go to the nearest post office to pick their parcel up.

These problems are similar to the ones reported in the literature and helped to frame the objective and goals of this book (see Sect. 1.2).

2.4 Final Remarks

This chapter presented an overview of the concepts of Smart Cities. Aspects such as how involving people in the development of smart solutions and digital ethics were highlighted. A focus to this book was also given, as the specific area of Smart Logistics and the problems in the last-mile delivery were studied. Furthermore, the specific needs of one of the partner companies that supported the development of this research work were also described.

Furthermore, the literature studied highlights a need to develop solutions that enable digital transformation and follow a digital-ethical behavior, even in traditional sectors such as the delivery industry. The authors such as Floridi (2018) had manifested that the new digital solutions should not only answer the questions *what is new?* or *what comes next?* but instead they should be directed toward building the next generation of *human-centered projects* for the digital age.

Unfortunately, most of the current efforts are directed toward using precise models that require precise data. Thus, this endeavor focuses on using approximate methods that enable making a decision under uncertainty, with reasonably good results. In the next chapter, such methods are studied more in detail.

---

[2] https://www.facebook.com/events/468651496930878/.

2.5 Further Readings

- **Meier and Portmann (2017)** "With this book, the editors provide a comprehensive overview of the use of information and communication technologies in cities and urban areas in order to sustainably develop social and ecological living spaces. Corresponding initiatives are summarized under the term Smart City" (abs.).
- **Portmann et al. (2019)** "The series *Studies in Systems, Decision and Control (SSDC)* covers both new developments and advances, as well as the state of the art, in the various areas of broadly perceived systems, decision making and control–quickly, up to date and with a high quality" (abs.).
- **Mańdziuk (2018)** "This paper presents an overview of recent advances in the field of the vehicle routing problem (VRP), based on papers published in high-quality journals during the period from January 2015 to July 2017" (abs.).
- **Korczak and Kijewska (2019)** "The challenges posed by Industry 4.0 serve as a motivation to introduce changes in practically all the areas: the organizational, production technology and social area. The dynamics of the increase of the use of IoT, CPS or SF and the benefits which are obtained by stakeholders have caused these solutions to find their practical applications in other areas of our lives including urbanized areas (cities)" (abs.).

References

Andreasyan, N., Dorado, A. F. D., Colombo, M., Teran, L., Pincay, J., Nguyen, M. T., & Portmann, E. (2021). Framework for involving citizens in human smart city projects using collaborative events. In *2021 Eighth International Conference on eDemocracy eGovernment (ICEDEG)* (pp. 103–109).

Benevolo, C., Dameri, R. P., & D'auria, B. (2016). Smart mobility in smart city. In *Empowering organizations* (pp. 13–28). Springer.

Cohen, B. (2015). The smart city wheel. https://www.smart-circle.org/smartcity/blog/boyd-cohen-the-smart-city-wheel/, accessed: 2020-02-04.

Colombo, M., Hurle, S., Portmann, E., & Schäfer, E. (2020a). A framework for a crowdsourced creation of smart city wheels. In *2020 Seventh International Conference on eDemocracy and eGovernment (ICEDEG)* (pp. 305–308). IEEE.

Dyer, M., Corsini, F., & Certomà, C. (2017). Making urban design a public participatory goal: toward evidence-based urbanism. *Proceedings of the Institution of Civil Engineers-Urban Design and Planning, 170*, 173–186.

Estellés-Arolas, E., & González-Ladrón-de Guevara, F. (2012). Towards an integrated crowdsourcing definition. *Journal of Information science, 38*, 189–200.

Floridi, L. (2018). Soft ethics and the governance of the digital. *Philosophy and Technology, 31*, 1–8.

Jabeur, N., Al-Belushi, T., Mbarki, M., & Gharrad, H. (2017). Toward leveraging smart logistics collaboration with a multi-agent system based solution. *Procedia Computer Science, 109*, 672–679.

Korczak, J., & Kijewska, K. (2019). Smart logistics in the development of smart cities. *Transportation Research Procedia, 39*, 201–211.

Mańdziuk, J. (2018). New shades of the vehicle routing problem: Emerging problem formulations and computational intelligence solution methods. *IEEE Transactions on Emerging Topics in Computational Intelligence, 3,* 230–244.

Mangiaracina, R., Perego, A., Seghezzi, A., & Tumino, A. (2019). Innovative solutions to increase last-mile delivery efficiency in b2c e-commerce: A literature review. *International Journal of Physical Distribution and Logistics Management, 49,* 901–920.

Meier, A., & Portmann, E. (2017). *Smart City: Strategie, Governance und Projekte.* Springer.

Mieg, H. A. (2013). Einleitung: Perspektiven der stadtforschung. In *Stadt* (pp. 1–14). Springer.

Painter, M., Pouryousefi, S., Hibbert, S., & Russon, J. A. (2019). Sharing vocabularies: Towards horizontal alignment of values-driven business functions. *Journal of Business Ethics, 155,* 965–979.

Pan, S., Giannikas, V., Han, Y., Grover-Silva, E., & Qiao, B. (2017). Using customer-related data to enhance e-grocery home delivery. *Industrial Management and Data Systems, 117,* 1917–1933.

Papoutsis, K., & Nathanail, E. (2016). Facilitating the selection of city logistics measures through a concrete measures package: A generic approach. *Transportation Research Procedia, 12,* 679–691.

Pincay, J., Mensah, A., Portmann, E., & Terán, L. (2020). Forecasting travel times with space partitioning methods. In *Proceedings of the 6th International Conference on Geographical Information Systems Theory, Applications and Management—GISTAM* (pp. 151–159). INSTICC, SciTePress.

Pincay, J., Mensah, A. O., Portmann, E., & Terán, L. (2020a). Partitioning space to identify en-route movement patterns. In *2020 Seventh International Conference on eDemocracy and eGovernment (ICEDEG)* (pp. 43–49). IEEE.

Pletscher, C., Regli, S., Cueni, R., Golliard, T., & Portmann, E. (2016). Smarte logistik-und mobilitätslösungen für die stadt der zukunft: Entwicklungsbeispiele der schweizerischen post. In *Smart City* (pp. 167–184). Springer.

Portmann, E., Tabacchi, M. E., Seising, R., & Habenstein, A. (2019). *Designing cognitive cities.* Springer.

Seghezzi, A., Mangiaracina, R., Tumino, A., & Perego, A. (2021). 'pony express' crowdsourcing logistics for last-mile delivery in b2c e-commerce: An economic analysis. *International Journal of Logistics Research and Applications, 24,* 456–472.

Terán, L., Pincay, J., Wallimann-Helmer, I., & Portmann, E. (2021). A literature review on digital ethics from a humanistic and sustainable perspective. In *Proceedings of the 14th International Conference on Theory and Practice of Electronic Governance.* ICEGOV 2021, Association for Computing Machinery.

Tsampoulatidis, I., Ververidis, D., Tsarchopoulos, P., Nikolopoulos, S., Kompatsiaris, I., & Komninos, N. (2013). ImproveMyCity: An open source platform for direct citizen-government communication. In *Proceedings of the 21st ACM international conference on Multimedia* (pp. 839–842).

Uckelmann, D. (2008). A definition approach to smart logistics. In *International Conference on Next Generation Wired/Wireless Networking* (pp. 273–284). Springer.

Van Duin, J., De Goffau, W., Wiegmans, B., Tavasszy, L., & Saes, M. (2016). Improving home delivery efficiency by using principles of address intelligence for b2c deliveries. *Transportation Research Procedia, 12,* 14–25.

Van Woensel, T. (2012). Smart logistics. *Inaugural Lecture presented on March, 23.*

Wang, Y., Zheng, Y., & Xue, Y. (2014). Travel time estimation of a path using sparse trajectories. In *Proceedings of the 20th ACM SIGKDD international conference on Knowledge discovery and data mining* (pp. 25–34).

Zhang, Z., Wang, Y., Chen, P., He, Z., & Yu, G. (2017). Probe data-driven travel time forecasting for urban expressways by matching similar spatiotemporal traffic patterns. *Transportation Research Part C: Emerging Technologies, 85,* 476–493.

Chapter 3
Computational Intelligence

3.1 Overview of Fuzzy Logic Approaches

Fuzzy set theory is one of the main enablers of Computational Intelligence for computer systems (Abele and D'Onofrio (2020); Kramer (2009)). This section presents approaches of fuzzy logic, specifically the fuzzy sets theory (Zadeh et al., 1996). At its core, membership functions define fuzzy sets; fuzzy sets can be of a different order (i.e., generalization of traditional fuzzy sets) to model imprecision in a better manner. Furthermore, fuzzy sets are the base to define the concept of Linguistic Variable; with linguistic variables, one can extract summarizations from text and create Fuzzy Rules to perform inferences. These inferences follow the way people reason and have different models (e.g., functional and logical models) and can be used to implement decision systems for instance.

Figure 3.1 illustrates how these concepts interrelate. Furthermore, this section describes how fuzzy theory can be leveraged to address inaccuracy and uncertainty of traffic- and user-related data to enable the implementation of Smart Logistic solutions.

3.1.1 Fuzzy Sets Theory

A *set* is defined as a collection of elements that share the same properties. Such properties are used to define boundaries and differentiate the elements. Nevertheless, these boundaries cannot always be sharply defined in all cases. For instance, a customer of a postal service can have a defined set of booked products, but if the postal company wants to know all the customers with the *most potential* to purchase a new product, then the boundaries become blurry.

Fuzzy set theory emerged as a way of reasoning with imprecise predicates and finding appropriate representation of "blurry boundaries" between sets; they can be

J. Pincay Nieves, *Smart Urban Logistics*, Fuzzy Management Methods,
https://doi.org/10.1007/978-3-031-16704-1_3

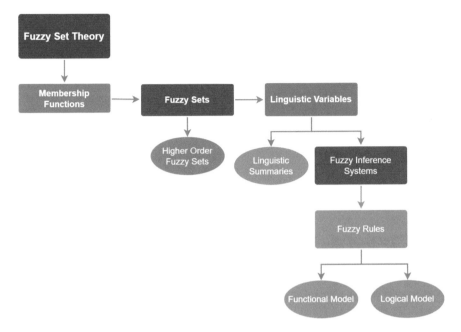

Fig. 3.1 Fuzzy sets theory concepts and their relationships

considered a generalization of traditional sets. Fuzzy sets thus are the base of fuzzy logic which facilitates the common sense reasoning (Zadeh, 1975).

Formally, a *fuzzy set* can be defined as follows (Pedrycz, 2020):

Definition 3.1 A fuzzy set A is described by a membership function mapping the elements of a universe X to the unit interval [0,1]:

$$A : X \to [0, 1] \tag{3.1}$$

which means that the membership functions depict the degree of belongingness of one element to a set, with a value of 0 implying complete exclusion and 1 meaning complete membership.

For example, if two sets are defined: *regular customers* for customers who performed at least five purchases during the last month and *occasional customers* for customers who have purchased less than five products but more than zero; when customer *XYZ* performed four purchases during the last month, then they would be classified as an *occasional customer* following the traditional set theory. This will be the same category of someone that performed only one transaction. If a fuzzy approach is followed, then the customer *XYZ* will belong in a certain degree to the *regular customers* set and with a complementary degree to the *occasional customer* set, which fits more the reality as the customer *XYZ* is *almost* a regular customer.

According to Pedrycz (2020), membership functions can be considered as synonyms of fuzzy sets, and they generalize characteristic functions in the same manner as fuzzy sets generalize sets. The membership functions should reflect the semantics of the concept to be represented, and they should be representative of the problem that is being addressed (Hudec, 2016; Pedrycz, 2020).

In the following sections, the different types of membership functions are explained.

3.1.1.1 Types of Membership functions

Membership functions are of two kinds: linear and Gaussian (Pedrycz, 2020).

Triangular membership functions: These functions are defined by a lower limit a, an upper limit b, and a modal value m also known as *prototype*. The prototype corresponds to the element with a membership degree of 1.

$$A(x; a, m, b) = \begin{cases} 0, & if \ x \le a \\ \frac{x-a}{m-a}, & if \ x \in [a, m] \\ \frac{b-x}{b-m}, & if \ x \in [m, b] \\ 0, & if \ x \ge b \end{cases} \quad (3.2)$$

Gaussian membership functions: These functions are defined by a modal value m and width σ as

$$A(x; m, \sigma) = e^{-(x-m)^2)/\sigma^2} \quad (3.3)$$

Trapezoidal membership functions: These functions are represented by a lower limit a, an upper limit b, and a flat segment $[m, n]$ which represents the highest value as

$$A(x; a, m, b) = \begin{cases} 0, & if \ x \le a \\ \frac{x-a}{m-a}, & if \ x \in [a, m] \\ 1, & if \ x \in [m, n] \\ \frac{b-x}{b-m}, & if \ x \in [n, b] \\ 0, & if \ x \ge b \end{cases} \quad (3.4)$$

Other types of membership functions are S-membership functions, piecewise membership functions, and singleton (Hudec, 2016; Pedrycz, 2020). Further types are S- and Z-functions for relaxing (smoothing) triangular membership functions and Pi Function for relaxing trapezoidal fuzzy sets (Keller et al., 2016). Figure 3.2 depicts graphically some examples of the most common membership functions.

Furthermore, membership functions are meant to enable expressing the uncertainty and concepts of a problem. Thus, if they are not adequately defined, the system most likely will not work correctly. To that effect, some constraints and design considerations that help assess if fuzzy sets are properly designed exist. In Sect. 3.1.5, some of such design criteria and constraint are introduced and explained.

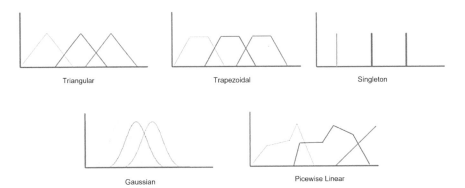

Triangular   Trapezoidal   Singleton

Gaussian   Picewise Linear

Fig. 3.2 Examples of membership functions

The next section introduces notions about higher order fuzzy sets, specifically Type-2 Fuzzy Sets (T2 FS). This type of fuzzy set is an extension of traditional fuzzy sets to handle uncertainty and incompleteness in a more suitable manner.

3.1.1.2   Type-2 Fuzzy Sets

Sometimes defining the boundaries of the fuzzy sets is not an easy task given the randomness and uncertainty of measured data (Li et al., 2006, 2016). To address that issue, the concept of Type-2 Fuzzy Sets was proposed by Zadeh (1975) and further studied by Mendel (2007).

T2 FSs were introduced as an extension of traditional fuzzy sets as an alternative to deal with uncertain membership criteria and parameters. Unlike type-1 fuzzy sets, the membership grades of a T2 FS are fuzzy sets themselves instead of crisp values. Mendel (2007) refers to type-2 fuzzy sets as "fuzzy-fuzzy sets that are convenient when the membership functions for a fuzzy set are hard to determine, being one example of this the modeling of words." Formally, a type-2 fuzzy set is defined as follows (Li et al., 2016; Zadeh, 1975):

Definition 3.2 A type-2 fuzzy set $\tilde{A}$ is characterized by its membership function $\mu_{\tilde{A}}(x, u)$, where $x \in X$ and $u \in J_x \subseteq [0, 1]$, that is to say

$$\tilde{A} = ((x, u), \mu_{\tilde{A}}(x, u)) \mid \forall x \in X, \forall u \in J_x \subseteq [0, 1]$$

where $0 \leq \mu_{\tilde{A}}(x, u) \leq 1$

T2 FS can also be understood as regions and not as a curve or discrete points as in the case of type-1 fuzzy sets. This characteristic enables to handle in better way randomness and uncertainty in the data.

However, computations with type-2 fuzzy sets are complex. Thus, most practical implementations and data modeling are done through one special kind of type-2

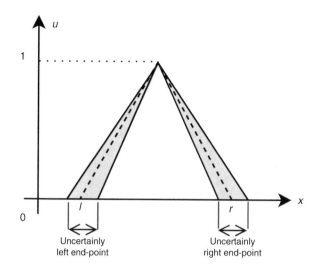

Fig. 3.3 Triangular membership functions depicting a type-2 fuzzy set as depicted in Pincay et al. (2021a)

fuzzy set called Interval Type-2 Fuzzy Sets (IT2 FS). Interval type-2 fuzzy set assume a uniform variation of the weighting of the parameters over the whole set; in this way, computations are less intense, and still, the capabilities to process randomness in data are kept (Li et al., 2016; Mendel, 2007). The following definition of IT2 FS is adopted (Li et al., 2016).

Definition 3.3 Membership grades of every element in type-2 fuzzy sets are type-1 fuzzy sets. If secondary membership grades are equal to 1, the set is an Interval Type-2 Fuzzy Sets (IT2 FS).

Figure 3.3 presents an example of an IT2 FS; note the so-called Footprint of Uncertainty (FOU), which corresponds to the uncertainty on the left and right end points. The uniformity observed on the FOU is due to the fact that the figure depicts an IT2 FS.

Moreover, according to Pedrycz (2020), two considerations need to be taken into account to decide when to use T2 FS. Firstly, the need to apply them must be clear, and their use should be straightforward, and secondly, there is a sound membership definition procedure that grants the definition of the fuzzy sets. Pedrycz (2020) also proposes an example that illustrates how to deal with the considerations above; in the case of having several datasets coming from different regions that present the influence of locality, they likely have some variability. Through T2 FS, this variability can be better captured, and the result of the aggregation of the datasets can be more faithful to reality.

Traffic-related data are used in the development of this project. Transportation and traffic parameters are defined in uncertain, imprecise, ambiguous, and subjective terms (Aftabuzzaman, 2007; Teodorović, 1994). The way T2 FSs enable handling uncertainty when defining fuzzy sets and performing inferences makes them suitable to study traffic-related variables and perform the developments intended in this research work.

Fuzzy sets help to represent natural phenomena and concepts that otherwise are difficult to capture. Such concepts can be used to perform operations, and to that end, the notion of linguistic variables was defined (Pedrycz, 2020). Linguistic variables help to describe situations or conditions in more human-like ways. The end goal is to enable computations and inferences under uncertainty. The conceptions around linguistic variables are presented next.

3.1.2   Linguistic Variables

Human beings describe situations and phenomena using words. For instance, if one asks another person *how cold is outside?* the other person could answer *very cold* or *not so cold* instead of providing an exact number describing the temperature.

Such a way of describing some characteristics can be leveraged to perform computations and extract knowledge under uncertainty. That brings the concept of *linguistic variable*, which enables computing with words (Pedrycz, 2020). In practical terms, linguistic variables are variables whose values are words expressed in natural language and are primarily combinations of adverbs (e.g., most of, some, and always) and adjectives (e.g., critical, warm, and tall). Linguistic variables are possible thanks to the concepts behind fuzzy sets and membership functions.

Formally, a linguistic variable is defined by a quintuple $(L, T(L), X, G, H)$, where L corresponds to the variable name, $T(L)$ is the set of all linguistic labels related to L, X depicts the universe of discourse of the variable, G is the syntactic rule to generate $T(L)$ which involves linguistic modifiers and logic operators, and H describes the semantic rule that relates each label $T(L)$ to its meaning $H(L)$, with $H(L)$ being a subset (membership function) of X.

As an example, let us consider the linguistic variable of speed on a highway and map the concepts to the elements described before:

- $L =$ speed on a highway.
- $T(L) = low, medium, high$. They represent the possible labels to describe the speed.
- $X = [0, 120]$, representing all the possible values of speed on the highway.
- G could be, for example, *very* or *not* (e.g., very low, not high).
- H is an example family of fuzzy sets depicted in Fig. 3.4.

It must be highlighted that linguistic variables depict perceptions and concepts, and as such, perceptions vary from person to person or are dependant on a particular situation. Thus, the most appropriate representation has to be found either based on the available data or even asking potential users of a system. There are, however, some design criteria and constraints that help to define linguistic variables. They are presented in detail in Sect. 3.1.5.

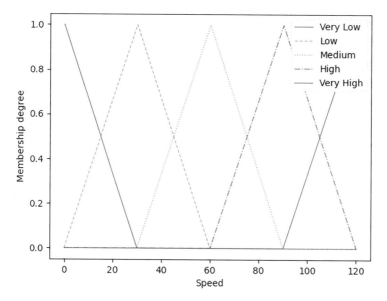

Fig. 3.4 Example of terms of the linguistic variable $L = speed\ on\ a\ highway$ over the universe of discourse $X = [0, 120]$

Furthermore, linguistic variables have a crucial role in developing intelligent systems as they are the base to develop linguistic summarizations over data and implement inference systems. In the case of traffic and smart logistics, linguistic variables can be helpful when depicting concepts as to how critical the traffic is at certain times of the day and change the driver's route depending on the circumstances. The details about linguistic summaries and fuzzy inference are presented in Sects. 3.1.3 and 3.1.4, respectively.

3.1.3 Linguistic Summaries

Linguistic summaries were first introduced by Yager (1982) as a way of summarizing data based on fuzzy theories. They respond to the need of providing summarized knowledge from data to users in an understandable manner through the use of linguistic terms (Hudec, 2016; Yager, 1982).

Certainly, statistic measures such as mean, median, and standard deviation help people to convey information; nevertheless, they limit the audience to a smaller set of specialized people.

Formally, a linguistic summary or summarizer S is expressed as

$$Qx(P(x)) \tag{3.5}$$

where Qx corresponds to a linguistic quantifier and $P(x)$ is a predicate describing evaluated attributes (Hudec et al., 2020; Kacprzyk & Zadrożny, 2005).

The aforementioned can be illustrated with the sentence *Most traffic accidents produce long time delays.* The term *most* is a linguistic quantifier, referring in this case to the majority of accidents; on the other hand, *long* is the predicate that describes the attribute time delay.

However, it is crucial to measure the validity of such sentences when mining them from large datasets. To that end, the validity (truth value) of a linguistic summary is defined as (Kacprzyk & Zadrozny, 2009)

$$v(Qx(P(x))) = \mu_Q \left(\frac{1}{n} \sum_{i=1}^{n} \mu_S(x_i) \right) \tag{3.6}$$

where n is the cardinality of a set, the expression $\frac{1}{n} \sum_{i=1}^{n} \mu_S(x_i)$ is the proportion of entities that meet the predicate P and μ_Q and μ_P, on the other hand, formalize the quantifier Q and predicate P through membership functions. The validity $v(Qx(P(x)))$ is thus a value from the unit interval.

Linguistic summaries are being widely used in Smart City solutions to inform citizens and not specialized audiences about the development of aspects in their cities. They constitute a promising way of extracting knowledge in an efficient fashion that fits in a better way how human beings think and express themselves (Boran et al., 2016; Hudec, 2019).

Moreover, from a technical perspective, data summarization is one of the basic capabilities that any intelligent system must have (Kacprzyk & Zadrozny, 2009), and thus, their inclusion as enhancement of applications of any kind is coherent.

3.1.4 Fuzzy Inference

Day to day, human beings perform inferences with uncertain information. For instance, *IF we have a bit of time AND it is not raining, THEN we can go to the mountain.* In this assertion, the antecedents and consequents are expressed by linguistic terms, and to be formed, they do not need precise information.

The details about how fuzzy logic supports such an inference process are presented next.

3.1.4.1 Fuzzy Inference and Fuzzy Rules

In principle, inference consists of deriving conclusions from premises, based on *modus ponens* in the form of IF-THEN rules (Hudec, 2016; Klir & Yuan, 1995):

$$p \Rightarrow q \tag{3.7}$$

where p constitutes a fact or antecedent, $p \Rightarrow q$ is a rule, and q is the conclusion. Such a conclusion will be either 1 or 0 (true or false).

In the fuzzy world, reasoning derives from a set of more flexible IF-THEN rules. Antecedents and consequents can also be fuzzy values or linguistic variables and not only depict crisp values. For instance, (fuzzy) rules can be expressed in the following manner:

$$IF \ x \ is \ A' \ THEN \ y \ is \ B' \tag{3.8}$$

where A' and B' are fuzzy sets for the antecedent and consequent, respectively, and the truth values will be in the interval [0, 1] instead of only 0 or 1. For instance, with fuzzy rules, one can perform the following reasoning *IF cars are slow THEN, there is most likely a traffic jam*; in this rule, the linguistic term *slow* can be represented through a fuzzy set and the quantifier *most likely* as well.

Fuzzy rules are the bridge that enables the forming of knowledge from individual pieces of information. They help to elicit a problem, represent and process knowledge, and produce a conclusion (Pedrycz, 2020). However, since the antecedents and consequents are not crisp values, the inference process is less straightforward than traditional inference models. Thus, Fuzzy Inference Systems exist, and they are presented in the following section.

3.1.4.2 Fuzzy Inference Systems

Fuzzy inference systems are computing frameworks that enable reaching a conclusion applying concepts of fuzzy sets, linguistic variables, and fuzzy rules. They are also known as fuzzy logic controllers or fuzzy expert systems (Hudec, 2016).

Two well-established fuzzy computing frameworks are the Mamdani and Sugeno models. The details are provided in the following:

- *Mamdani Model (Logical Model):* For this model, inputs and consequents come in the form of fuzzy sets that express linguistic terms or labels. Since the output of this process is a fuzzy set, a defuzzification (i.e., converting a fuzzy number to a crisp one) method should be used.
  Rules in a Mamdani system have the form:

$$IF \ x_1 \ is \ A'_1 \ AND...AND \ x_n \ is \ A'_n \ THEN \ y \ is \ B' \tag{3.9}$$

Furthermore, the inference process is conducted following the so-called Mamdani method of inference (see Mamdani 1974). Advantages of this model include that it is well suited to human input and highly expressive, while their main disadvantages are that the size of a rule base increases with the number of input attributes and linguistic terms and more intense computations due to the defuzzification process.

- *Sugeno Model (Functional Model):* This model is similar to the likes of the Mamdani model. The antecedents are the same (i.e., they represent linguistic terms or fuzzy sets), but the consequent is either a constant or a linear function. Thus, the rules have the following form:

$$IF\ x_1\ is\ A'_1\ AND...AND\ x_n\ is\ A'_n\ THEN\ y = a_1 x_y + .. + a_n X_x + c$$

$$(3.10)$$

where a_n is the i_{th} coefficient in the r_{th} rule and c is a constant. The output of a Sugeno rule is computed using a weighted average model, while the inference is performed used a rule weight method (see Sugeno and Kang 1988). The advantages of the Sugeno model include its suitability to perform mathematical analysis and that it is not necessary to perform a defuzzification process to the output, which reduces the processing times. Among its disadvantages is that it might be further from the way humans perform reasoning, and thus, there could be a loss of interpretability.

Regarding which model to use when building a fuzzy inference system, the answer depends on the context and application of the system. If it is more targeted to resemble humans' reasoning, then the Mamdani model might be the best answer. On the contrary, if the application is directed toward performing mathematical simulations, then the Sugeno Model could be more appropriate. Moreover, if the system designers cannot perform a defuzzification process, the answer is clear.

In terms of constraints when designing a fuzzy inference system, they include consistency, average firing rules, and completeness. All of them related to keep the number of rules as low as possible, cover all the possible cases, and avoid firing many of them with one input (Moral et al., 2021). Such criteria become more critical as the system grows and needs to perform inferences with more data. More details are provided next.

3.1.5 Design Criteria and Constraints for Fuzzy Systems

A fuzzy system should be *interpretable*. With interpretability, it is meant that when a human inspects a system, they should be able to understand their engine and how inferences are performed. Several authors use the terms transparency and comprehensibility in the literature as synonyms for interpretability (Moral et al., 2021).

Some criteria and constraints need to be considered when designing an interpretable fuzzy system. However, as manifested by Moral et al. (2021), there is no consensus about a defined set of constraints and criteria that need to be accomplished to achieve a certain level of interpretability; they are more of the kind of design options led by specific requirements.

Furthermore, fuzzy systems are meant to enable the expression of uncertainty and concepts related to a problem. Fuzzy sets, linguistic variables, family of fuzzy sets, and fuzzy inference systems need to be properly defined to ensure the aforementioned. The following sections introduce some constraints and criteria that need to be taken into account when designing interpretable fuzzy systems.

3.1.5.1 Design Criteria and Constraints for Fuzzy Sets

The following are constraints and criteria that need to be taken into account when designing interpretable fuzzy sets (Moral et al., 2021):

(i) *Normality:* By this concept it is meant that each fuzzy set contains at least one element with a membership degree of 1. That element is a *prototype* or core of a fuzzy set.

(ii) *Continuity:* Since fuzzy sets model perception-based concepts, the membership functions depicting such perceptions should be continuous in the universe of discourse. Such constraint results from the assertion that humans perceive the environment as continuously varying.

(iii) *Convexity:* This criterion implies that the membership values of elements belonging to any interval must not be lower than the membership values of the boundaries of the function.

These design criteria and constraints are fine when defining single fuzzy sets. However, normally systems require multiple sets to define linguistic variables and create a frame of cognition and inference. In the following, design criteria for such cases are presented.

3.1.5.2 Design Criteria for Linguistic Variables

A family of fuzzy sets (i.e., frame of cognition) $A = \{A_1, A_2, \ldots, A_c\}$ must provide a comprehensive description of a variable over a space or universe of discourse X. When defining each of the fuzzy sets, they need to express well-formed semantics and are experimentally justifiable (Pedrycz & Wang, 2015). Furthermore, when dealing with natural language, it is crucial to maintain the linguistic variables meaningful to the end-user. Thus, constructs that might not mean anything to a person must be avoided, for example, *very very medium*.

To avoid such situations, some design criteria and constraints when defining linguistic variables are presented in the following (Moral et al., 2021):

(i) *Limited number of fuzzy sets:* The maximal number of fuzzy sets in A should not exceed 9. Otherwise, it does not meet the goal of representing reality in an accurate manner as a person might have problems distinguishing between *very bad* and *very very bad* for example.

(ii) *Relation preservation:* The defined fuzzy sets and their labels must keep a proper ordering of the concept depicted. For example, a linguistic variable with labels $T(L) = \{medium, low, very\ high, high\}$ might not properly depict an evident relationship of concepts.

(iii) *Justifiable number of elements:* The number of terms of linguistic terms in a linguistic variable should not be too high and kept less than 7 ± 2.

(iv) *Distinguishability:* The different labels or terms of a linguistic variable should be represented by well-distinguishable fuzzy sets. This implies that fuzzy sets with too much overlap would not be representing different concepts but the same one. Also, a low overlapping is a sign of possible issues in the design of the fuzzy sets.

(v) *Coverage:* Each element of the universe of discourse should be well represented by at least one fuzzy set or label of a linguistic variable.

(vi) *Complementarity:* The fuzzy partition in a linguistic variable should form a strong fuzzy partition, meaning that the sets are all normal and convex. In other words, no more than two fuzzy sets should have a nonzero membership value for an element of the universe of discourse.

(vii) *Uniform granulation:* This implies that the cardinality (i.e., the area bounded by a membership function or fuzzy set) of all fuzzy sets in a linguistic variable should be almost the same.

(viii) *Leftmost/rightmost fuzzy sets:* This constraint means that the lower and upper bounds of a fuzzy set ought to be prototypes for some other fuzzy set of the linguistic variable.

(ix) *Natural partitioning:* This constraint implies that if some elements of the universe of discourse have a special meaning, then each of those elements should be a prototype of some fuzzy set in the linguistic variable.

(x) *Unimodality:* This means that the membership functions have at least one modal value.

Lastly, as explained in Sect. 3.1.4, rules are the core of fuzzy inference systems. Thus, it is coherent to think that some design criteria for them also exist. In the following, section some of these criteria are presented.

3.1.5.3   Design Criteria and Constraints for Fuzzy Rules

Rules represent a piece of knowledge. In the fuzzy world, it represents the relationship between information granules and fosters the integration of knowledge.

A clear structure of a fuzzy rule leads to more interpretable and explainable systems. Some design criteria and constraints for its design include (Moral et al., 2021):

(i) *Rule length:* The length of the rule should be as small as possible.

(ii) *Local models:* The consequent of a rule should describe a model with a good precision, meaning that the consequent has to be immediately understandable by considering the antecedents.

(iii) *Granular consequents:* Rule outputs should be represented by linguistic terms.

Moreover, an interpretable fuzzy system eases adjusting an existing model to other contexts by adjusting parameters. For instance, a fuzzy system designed for a company operating in different regions, an interpretable fuzzy system, is straightforward to adapt to the specificity of each of the regions where the company operates (Mináriková, 2021).

In this research project, all of these design criteria and constraints are followed in the proposed solutions' conception.

3.2 Swarm Intelligence

The concept of swarm intelligence denotes the collective intelligence that agents, interacting in a multi-agent system, exhibit to achieve an objective. Typically, such agents collaborate with others to find knowledge. These agents can be modeled artificially by observing the behavior of social insects in nature, such as ants and bees.

Generalities about swarm intelligence and details about two swarm intelligence algorithms, the Ant Colony Optimization (ACO) and the Fuzzy Ant System (FAS), are presented in this section. ACO is a swarm intelligence method (and thus also a CI method) inspired by how ants behave in nature to find the best routes to obtain food. These simple organisms are able to organize themselves to find the best paths to retrieve their food from a source to their nests. Such capability has been leveraged in the implementation of computational methods toward finding a solution to optimization problems. On the other hand, FAS can be considered as the combination of ACO with fuzzy logic to deal with the uncertainty that an optimization problem brings along.

Thus, this section describes the basics of swarm intelligence in Sect. 3.2.1 and introduces in Sect. 3.2.2 the Ant Colony Optimization (ACO) principles and how they can be used to solve traffic-related problems. Section 3.2.3 describes how fuzzy concepts can be applied to ACO to represent more accurately natural phenomena. Finally, Sect. 3.2.4 presents the current challenges and trends in this research field.

3.2.1 Basics of Swarm Intelligence

Many problems in nature cannot be effectively modeled given their complex behavior. One example of them is traffic congestion. Traffic results from the interplay of multiple behaviors from different vehicles and other factors, and thus, it is a complex problem to predict.

As a way of addressed the above-mentioned issues, the *agent-based modeling* was conceptualized as a way of understanding how each *agent* (e.g.., vehicles and people) interacts with others to obtain the overall image of a system (Teodorović, 2008). Examples of such agents in traffic and transportation matters include drivers, travelers, and other economic entities.

On the other hand, social insects such as bees, ants, and wasps exhibit a behavior characterized by acting autonomously while self-organizing themselves and interacting to achieve a goal. This conduct has inspired the researchers to use the *swarm intelligence* concept to develop artificial agent-based systems to solve a variety of problems. Particular interest has been given to how the insects communicate; for instance, the bees dance around nectar sources, and ants leave a track of a substance called pheromone that signals their peers to act in one way or another. Such a communication system is denoted as the collective intelligence of the colonies. The term swarm intelligence also denotes such intelligence (Beni & Wang, 1993).

Swarm intelligence is thus a branch of artificial intelligence grounded on the behavior of individual agents in the solution of decentralized problems (Teodorović, 2008).

The agents acting in a swarm system could be intelligent or reactive. Intelligent means that the agents have some skills to collaborate with others and achieve goals. On the contrary, reactive agents are not intelligent, and they behave in response to different events or signals. In both cases, they are autonomous. Bees, ants, and wasps can be considered as reactive agents since they respond to stimuli coming from peer agents (Teodorović, 2008).

Furthermore, some examples of swarm intelligence algorithms are ant colony optimization, bee colony optimization, stochastic diffusion search, and swarm particle optimization. They had been applied successfully to a variety of optimization problems, including search, traffic, and scheduling.

Only the details about the ant colony optimization algorithm and its enhancement with fuzzy concepts (FAS) are presented in the following sections.

Swarm intelligence methods were chosen in the development of this work given its applicability in solving traffic-related and vehicle routing problems found in the literature (e.g., Jabbarpour et al. 2014; Mańdziuk 2018; Teodorović 2008).

3.2.2 Ant Colony Optimization

Optimization problems are relevant for practitioners and scholars. Some examples include scheduling problems or finding the best route to achieve a goal. Probably, the most known optimization problem is the Traveling Salesman Problem (TCP); a salesman has to visit several cities only one time while keeping the traveling distance at the minimum (Blum, 2005).

Diverse approaches exist to solve optimization problems. They can be either complete or approximate. Complete algorithms can find a solution to the optimization problem in a bounded time frame. However, not all problems can be optimized in a limited time, and thus approximate solutions aim at finding less optimal ones (but still good ones) in more reasonable time frames (Bell & Griffis, 2010; Blum, 2005). This type of solution has got special attention in recent years.

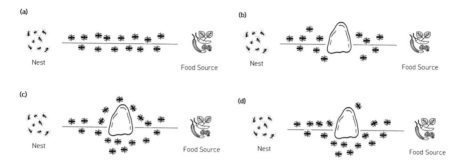

Fig. 3.5 Examples of ant behavior: (**a**) the ants follow a trail from their nest to a food source, (**b**) an obstacle forces them to find other routes, (**c**) some ants take one path, and others a different one, and (**d**) thanks for the strength of the pheromones the best path is discovered. Adapted from Teodorović (2008)[*]

[*]All icons included are from the thenounproject.com used under Creative Commons license

Ant colony optimization is one of the so-called approximate algorithms for optimizations. It is a metaheuristic that allows solving complex combinatorial optimization problems (Teodorović, 2008). It was first introduced in the 1990s by Dorigo (1992) and was defined upon observing the behavior of the ants in nature. Ants live in colonies, and to survive, they need to collaborate to find food and take it back to their nests. To do so, they leave a chemical pheromone trail when exploring a certain area. The next ants tend to choose the trails with the strongest pheromone concentration, leading them to find the shortest path from the source to the nest. Figure 3.5 depicts an example of such behavior.

Furthermore, ACO is considered as a swarm intelligence algorithm from the perspective of Artificial Intelligence (AI) (Blum, 2005; Tatomir & Rothkrantz, 2006).

Moreover, ACO has been applied successfully in different domains of routing problems. One example is the work of Durand and Alliot in which the authors attempted to optimize the solution of air traffic conflicts; He and Hou (2012) performed a study for traffic signal timing optimization using ant-based algorithms and obtained promising results. Further examples include the AntNet algorithm described in Di Caro and Dorigo (1998), which addresses the routing problem in packet-switched networks and the work of Jagadeesh et al. (2002) that introduced a hierarchical routing algorithm that computes a near-optimal route in an extensive city road network.

Even if there exist various shortest path and optimal route algorithms (e.g., Dijkstra, A* search algorithm, and Bellman-Ford algorithm) (Chen et al., 2014; Tatomir & Rothkrantz, 2006), they are relatively static and do not respond to the need of routing problems in dynamic environments where factors such as traffic conditions and weather play crucial roles when finding optimal routes. Thus, alternative solutions are needed.

The pseudocode for the ACO algorithm is presented in Algorithm 3.1. Basically, given a network, some ants are located on each node. For each cycle, an ant decides which node to move based on the pheromone intensity. The more intense the pheromone is, the more desirable certain path is to reach the next node. When an ant moves to the next node, the pheromone intensity has to be updated, implying that if an ant passed in the previous step, the pheromone intensity will last longer over time, and if an ant has not traversed a path, the pheromone trail in that segment is going to be weak meaning that it might not be the best path to go. The algorithm finishes when each ant has generated a solution, and other conditions are met (e.g., a determined number of cycles or time). In the end, the top-performing routes found by the ants are selected.

Algorithm 3.1 ACO algorithm in pseudocode

1: **while** Termination conditions are not met **do**
2:      Locate each ant in a starting node
3:      **repeat**
4:          **for** each ant **do**
5:              Choose the next node by applying a transition rule
6:              Update pheromone trail
7:          **end for**
8:      **until** Every ant has built a solution
9: **end while**
10: Determine the best solution(s) from the ones generated by the ants
11: **return** The best solution(s)

For instance, to solve the previously mentioned TCP with ACO, artificial ants correspond to the entities in charge of finding a solution in the solution space. At the beginning of the search (time $t = 0$), the ants are located in different towns (nodes) that need to be visited or served by the salesman; then, when an ant moves to an unvisited town, it leaves a pheromone (trail intensity) which helps other ants to decide the paths to choose in the future depending on the pheromone intensity (Teodorović, 2008). Moreover, the next movement or the so-called transition probability $p_{ij}^k(t)$ is defined by the following expression (Teodorović & Lučić, 2005, 2007):

$$p_{ij}^k(t) = \begin{cases} \dfrac{\tau_{ij}(t)^\alpha \eta_{ij}{}^\beta}{\sum_{h \in \Omega_i^k(t)} \tau_{ih}(t)^\alpha \eta_{ih}{}^\beta} & , if\ j \in \Omega_i^k(t) \\ 0 & , otherwise \end{cases} \tag{3.11}$$

where $\Omega_i^k(t)$ corresponds to all the possible nodes to be visited by an ant k, d_{ij} is the Euclidean distance between nodes i and j, τ_{ij} represents the pheromone along the link (i, j), $\eta_{ij} = 1/d_{ij}$ is the *visibility*, and α and β are parameters that represent the importance given to the trail pheromone intensity and visibility.

One crucial concept from the previous explanation is the one of *utility*. It refers to the desirability of choosing a node j while currently being on node i (Bonabeau et al., 1999), meaning that the utility is based on local information. In the case of pheromone trail intensity, the more importance it is given, the more desirable the link becomes, since that means that many ants have already passed that way (Teodorović, 2008). Moreover, every ant will complete a traveling salesman tour after *n* iterations; *m* iterations of the algorithm are called a cycle, and after each cycle, the trail intensity needs to be updated, following the natural behavior of evaporation of pheromones. There are different methods to update the trail intensity (see Bonabeau et al. 1999; Dorigo and Di Caro 1999; Teodorović 2008), and this is made to discover a suitable solution through cooperation.

3.2.3 Fuzzy Ant System Principles

Teodorović and Lučić (2005, 2007) went further from the traditional ACO and proposed the Fuzzy Ant System. FAS is the result of the combination of ACO with concepts of fuzzy logic. The principles are the same, differing on how the *utility* to visit the next node is calculated. The authors assumed that the ants can perceive the distance between nodes as *small*, *medium*, and *big*, whereas the trail intensity can be anticipated as *weak*, *medium*, or *strong*. Furthermore, an approximate rule of a reasoning algorithm to compute the utility when choosing the next link is composed of fuzzy rules similar to the following:

If d_{ij} is SMALL and τ_{ij} is STRONG
Then u_{ij} is VERY HIGH

where d_{ij} is the distance between node i and node j, τ_{ij} represents the pheromone along the link (i, j), and u_{ij} corresponds to the ant's utility when choosing the node j, considering that the ant is located in the node i. A reasoning algorithm of this nature is used to replace Eq. 3.11.

With fuzzy logic acting as a separate module within an ACO implementation is possible to handle the uncertainty present in complex combinatorial problems (Teodorović, 2008). Fuzzy rules reduce the complexity and enable the representation of nature and reality with higher fidelity, leading to the generation of exemplary implementations that can find solutions in a reasonable computational time (Teodorović & Lučić, 2005).

The basic FAS algorithm consists of deploying an *m* number of ants in a network and make them find the best set of routes from a start to a destination. The algorithm is executed in a determined number of cycles, and after all the cycles are completed, the top-performing routes are obtained. Algorithm 3.2 presents the pseudocode of the FAS proposed by Teodorović (2008).

Furthermore, FAS implementations have been successfully applied to scheduling, vehicle routing, and flow management problem. Thus, the application and adaptation of the FAS to address last-mile delivery issues are coherent.

Algorithm 3.2 FAS algorithm as proposed in Teodorović (2008)

1: Describe demand at the nodes by corresponding triangular fuzzy numbers. Set the counter of the cycles to zero ($c = 0$)
2: If the number of finished cycles c is equal to the assigned number of cycles, go to step 4. Otherwise, go to Step 3.
3: Set the counter of ants to one ($k = 1$). Locate all m ants in the depot. Generate m sets of routes by m ants. Generate routes using sequential approach (one ant at the time). When all nodes are visited, ant k will finish with the route design. Increase the ant counter by one after creating one set of the routes. If the ant counter is equal to $m + 1$, increase the cycle counter by one and go to step 2. In the opposite case allow next ant to create the set of routes within considered cycle.
4: **return** Take as the final solution such a set of routes that have the least total sum of planned route lengths and additional distance due to "route failure". End the algorithm.

3.2.4   Trends and Challenges in Swarm Intelligence Applications

This section provides an overview of the application of swarm intelligence algorithms in smart logistics and vehicle routing, current trends, and outlook and challenges.

3.2.4.1   Current Trends

Swarm intelligence algorithms are being applied in three major areas of research (Jabbarpour et al., 2014; Teodorović, 2008):

1. Vehicle routing and scheduling
2. Public transit
3. Traffic engineering and control

ACO algorithms have been used to find solutions to numerous Vehicle Routing Problem cases. Bullnheimer et al. (1999) were among the firsts who applied ant colony optimization to find the best routes to visit a set of customers. With the obtained results, the authors proved how using ant systems is feasible for VRP problems. Since then, most initiatives were targeted to use more colonies to obtain better results and combining ACO with other heuristics for scalability reasons. More recent publications are devoted to studying traffic flow modeling from different perspectives, such as the initiative of Poole and Kotsialos (2016), where the authors attempted to use swarm intelligence to analyze traffic flow in a macroscopic manner.

In public transit, most efforts are directed to finding better ways of designing road networks and improving public transit connections. Examples of publications in this area include the proposal of Teodorović and Lučić (2005) to improve the schedule synchronization in public transit using the Fuzzy Ant System. Another approach is the one of Ahmadi (2020) that aimed at redesigning the public transit network of the city of Sanandaj (Iran) to increase the usage of public transportation in the city.

Traffic engineering and control is also an area where swarm intelligence algorithms are being widely applied. Research in this area is oriented to improve traffic signaling and control to keep traffic flowing while avoiding traffic anomalies. The authors He and Hou (2012) used an ant colony-based algorithm to optimize the traffic signal timing to minimize the travel time delays and the number of stops of vehicles. Another related initiative is authored by García-Nieto et al. (2012), and they applied swarm intelligence methods to improve the cycle programs of traffic lights of the cities of Málaga and Sevilla (in Spain).

Some common points found in all these works are:

- They are targeted to improving traffic and circulation on roads and streets.
- They attempt to improve circulation by proposing new designs for road networks, public transport systems, and signaling control.
- Most implementations are theoretical.
- They are designed for specific scenarios or situations.

3.2.4.2 Outlook and Challenges

Improving the way people circulate on the roads and streets is a complex problem. The fact that traffic occurs under uncertain and dynamic situations (e.g., event such accidents, weather change, and a sudden increase of the number of vehicles) calls for methods that at least enable to approximate a solution under these special circumstances.

Swarm intelligence algorithms, and particularly ACO, have proven to be a suitable option to address the challenges that improving vehicle routing, transit, and traffic control brings along. The results obtained from the application and implementation of this metaheuristic demonstrate that it is a solid alternative toward appeasing the present and future problems of mobility.

However, many questions remain unanswered about the potential of swarm solutions in the transportation field.

- Their limitations need to be studied in depth. Most of the current studies highlight their advantages over other methods, but their limitations still are not being fully understood, especially when issues such as scalability remain unexplored.
- Their real potential should be fully explored. As per the results of previous efforts, swarm algorithms are promising. Nevertheless, they are not as widely used and applied as other artificial intelligence and machine learning techniques (e.g., neural networks).
- The combination with other theories and techniques (e.g., fuzzy set theory) needs to be widely analyzed and validated. The inspiration behind the swarm algorithm is social insects that do not exhibit some apparent "intelligence," but improving the artificial agents and making them capable to learn could help to solve more complex problems.

- They have been mostly applied to traffic and transport engineering, but there is a lack of development of frameworks that enable the improvement of services that use the roads (e.g., logistic and delivery services).

Addressing the abovementioned challenges could enable the conceptualization and implementation of new models to contribute not only theoretically but also practically in the improvement of transportation and logistics services.

3.3 Final Remarks

This chapter presented a review of theories that enable the implementation of systems that exhibit some degree of human or more biological capabilities.

Such methods are able to tolerate and handle in a better way the uncertainty and partial truth to convey knowledge than hard computing methods (Zadeh, 1996). Even if methods such as artificial intelligence and machine learning are widely used, offer good results, are investigated, and constantly improved, the concerns about the high energy consumption that the computers processing data for these methods remain (García-Martín et al., 2019). Thus, investigating and applying methods based on soft or approximate computing is coherent.

Furthermore, fuzzy concepts allow enhancing other methods such as the likes of the swarm intelligence to represent nature in a more accurate manner. As it was previously explained, it is closer to reality to represent the perception of distance as *short* or *long* instead of exact measurement, as specific instruments are needed to obtain them. This capability enables to use of data that otherwise will be discarded for being considered incomplete. Figure 3.6 exemplifies how through fuzziness swarm intelligence methods can be leveraged to solve problems with incomplete data.

The author of this work chose to apply and research computational intelligence methods mainly for the reasons mentioned above. Additionally, these methods can enable the development of more ethical solutions since, through approximation; there is no need for explicit data coming from constant tracking of people while still achieving reasonable levels of reliability.

In Chaps. 4 and 5, the details about the development of two applications with CI methods are presented. The results obtained affirm and illustrate how fuzzy methods allow the implementation of reliable tools while avoiding the usage of large amounts of data and computational-intensive methods.

3.4 Further Readings

- **Hudec (2016)** "This book explains the application of fuzzy approaches for classical relational databases and information systems. It details important

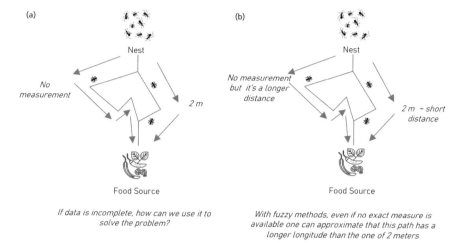

Fig. 3.6 Examples of how fuzzy methods can help to solve problems with incomplete data: (**a**) the distance of one path is unknown, and (**b**) the distance of the unknown path can be approximated to *long*[*]

[*] All icons included are from the thenounproject.com used under Creative Commons license

application aspects like fuzzy queries, fuzzy inference, and linguistic summaries. Includes a brief introduction to fuzzy sets and fuzzy logic" (abs.).

- **Moral et al. (2021)** "This book explains in details how fuzzy models can participate in the construction of decision systems. It also establishes a bridge with natural language processing and automatic text generation and it proposes solutions to deal with the well-known interpretability-accuracy trade-off and covers all aspects of interpretability of fuzzy rule-based systems, from interpretability rating to directly exploitable software" (abs.).

- **Dorigo and Di Caro (1999)** "Recently, a number of algorithms inspired by the foraging behavior of ant colonies have been applied to the solution of difficult discrete optimization problems. We put these algorithms in a common framework by defining the Ant Colony Optimization (ACO) meta-heuristic. A couple of paradigmatic examples of applications of these novel meta-heuristic are given, as well as a brief overview of existing applications" (abs.).

- **Teodorović (2008)** "Swarm intelligence is the branch of artificial intelligence based on study of behavior of individuals in various decentralized systems. The paper presents a classification and analysis of the results achieved using swarm intelligence to model complex traffic and transportation processes. The primary goal of this paper is to acquaint readers with the basic principles of Swarm Intelligence, as well as to indicate potential swarm intelligence applications in traffic and transportation" (abs.).

References

Abele, D., & D'Onofrio, S. (2020). Artificial intelligence–the big picture. In *Cognitive Computing* (pp. 31–65). Springer Vieweg, Wiesbaden.

Aftabuzzaman, M. (2007). Measuring traffic congestion-a critical review. In *Proceedings of the 30th Australasian transport research forum* (pp. 1–16).

Ahmadi, A. (2020). Transit network design using gis and ant colony optimization in sanandaj. *Journal of Geographic Information System, 12*, 646–662.

Bell, J. E., & Griffis, S. E. (2010). Swarm intelligence: Application of the ant colony optimization algorithm to logistics-oriented vehicle routing problems. *Journal of Business Logistics, 31*, 157–175.

Beni, G., & Wang, J. (1993). Swarm intelligence in cellular robotic systems. In *Robots and biological systems: towards a new bionics?* (pp. 703–712). Springer.

Blum, C. (2005). Ant colony optimization: Introduction and recent trends. *Physics of Life reviews, 2*, 353–373.

Bonabeau, E., Dorigo, M., Marco, D. d. R. D. F., Theraulaz, G., Théraulaz, G. et al. (1999). *Swarm intelligence: from natural to artificial systems* (Vol. 1). Oxford University Press.

Boran, F. E., Akay, D., & Yager, R. R. (2016). An overview of methods for linguistic summarization with fuzzy sets. *Expert Systems with Applications, 61*, 356–377.

Bullnheimer, B., Hartl, R. F., & Strauss, C. (1999). An improved ant system algorithm for thevehicle routing problem. *Annals of operations research, 89*, 319–328.

Chen, Y. z., Shen, S. f., Chen, T., & Yang, R. (2014). Path optimization study for vehicles evacuation based on dijkstra algorithm. *Procedia Engineering, 71*, 159–165.

Di Caro, G., & Dorigo, M. (1998). Antnet: Distributed stigmergetic control for communications networks. *Journal of Artificial Intelligence Research, 9*, 317–365.

Dorigo, M. (1992). Optimization, learning and natural algorithms [Ph. D. thesis]. In *Politecnico di Milano, Italy*.

Dorigo, M., & Di Caro, G. (1999). Ant colony optimization: A new meta-heuristic. In *Proceedings of the 1999 congress on evolutionary computation-CEC99 (Cat. No. 99TH8406)* (Vol. 2, pp. 1470–1477). IEEE.

Durand, N., & Alliot, J. M. (2009). Ant colony optimization for air traffic conflict resolution. In *ATM seminar 2009, 8th USA/Europe air traffic management research and developpment seminar*.

García-Martín, E., Rodrigues, C. F., Riley, G., & Grahn, H. (2019). Estimation of energy consumption in machine learning. *Journal of Parallel and Distributed Computing, 134*, 75–88.

García-Nieto, J., Alba, E., & Olivera, A. C. (2012). Swarm intelligence for traffic light scheduling: Application to real Urban areas. *Engineering Applications of Artificial Intelligence, 25*, 274–283.

He, J., & Hou, Z. (2012). Ant colony algorithm for traffic signal timing optimization. *Advances in Engineering Software, 43*, 14–18.

Hudec, M. (2016). Fuzziness in information systems. In *Springer International Publishing* (pp. 67–99).

Hudec, M. (2019). Possibilities for linguistic summaries in cognitive cities. In *Designing Cognitive Cities* (pp. 47–84). Springer.

Hudec, M., Vučetić, M., & Čermáková, I. (2020). The synergy of linguistic summaries, fuzzy functional dependencies and land coverings for augmenting informativeness in smart cities. In *2020 28th Telecommunications Forum (TELFOR)* (pp. 1–4). IEEE.

Jabbarpour, M. R., Jalooli, A., Shaghaghi, E., Noor, R. M., Rothkrantz, L., Khokhar, R. H., & Anuar, N. B. (2014). Ant-based vehicle congestion avoidance system using vehicular networks. *Engineering Applications of Artificial Intelligence, 36*, 303–319.

Jagadeesh, G. R., Srikanthan, T., & Quek, K. (2002). Heuristic techniques for accelerating hierarchical routing on road networks. *IEEE Transactions on Intelligent Transportation Systems, 3*, 301–309.

Kacprzyk, J., & Zadrożny, S. (2005). Linguistic database summaries and their protoforms: towards natural language based knowledge discovery tools. *Information Sciences, 173*, 281–304.

Kacprzyk, J., & Zadrozny, S. (2009). Protoforms of linguistic database summaries as a human consistent tool for using natural language in data mining. *International Journal of Software Science and Computational Intelligence (IJSSCI), 1*, 100–111.

Keller, J. M., Liu, D., & Fogel, D. B. (2016). *Fundamentals of computational intelligence: neural networks, fuzzy systems, and evolutionary computation.* Wiley.

Klir, G., & Yuan, B. (1995). *Fuzzy sets and fuzzy logic* (Vol. 4). Prentice Hall New Jersey.

Kramer, O. (2009). *Computational intelligence: Eine Einführung.* Springer.

Li, L., Lin, W. H., & Liu, H. (2006). Type-2 fuzzy logic approach for short-term traffic forecasting. In *IEE Proceedings-Intelligent Transport Systems* (Vol. 153, pp. 33–40). IET.

Li, R., Jiang, C., Zhu, F., & Chen, X. (2016). Traffic flow data forecasting based on interval type-2 fuzzy sets theory. *IEEE/CAA Journal of Automatica Sinica, 3*, 141–148.

Mamdani, E. H. (1974). Application of fuzzy algorithms for control of simple dynamic plant. In *Proceedings of the institution of electrical engineers* (Vol. 121, pp. 1585–1588). IET.

Mańdziuk, J. (2018). New shades of the vehicle routing problem: Emerging problem formulations and computational intelligence solution methods. *IEEE Transactions on Emerging Topics in Computational Intelligence, 3*, 230–244.

Mendel, J. M. (2007). Type-2 fuzzy sets and systems: an overview. *IEEE Computational Intelligence Magazine, 2*, 20–29.

Mináriková, E. (2021). Criteria for fuzzy rule-based systems and its applicability on examples. In *Proceedings of the 24th International Scientific Conference for Doctoral Students and Post-Doctoral Scholars (EDAMBA).* University of Economics in Bratislava.

Moral, J. M. A., Castiello, C., Magdalena, L., & Mencar, C. (2021). *Explainable Fuzzy Systems: Paving the way from Interpretable Fuzzy Systems to Explainable AI Systems.* Springer.

Pedrycz, W. (2020). *An Introduction to Computing with Fuzzy Sets: Analysis, Design, and Applications* (Vol. 190). Springer Nature.

Pedrycz, W., & Wang, X. (2015). Designing fuzzy sets with the use of the parametric principle of justifiable granularity. *IEEE Transactions on Fuzzy Systems, 24*, 489–496.

Pincay, J., Portmann, E., & Terán, L. (2021a). Fuzzifying geospatial data to identify critical traffic areas. In *Joint Proceedings of the 19th World Congress of the International Fuzzy Systems Association (IFSA), the 12th Conference of the European Society for Fuzzy Logic and Technology (EUSFLAT), and the 11th International Summer School on Aggregation Operators (AGOP)* (pp. 463–470). Atlantis Press.

Poole, A., & Kotsialos, A. (2016). Swarm intelligence algorithms for macroscopic traffic flow model validation with automatic assignment of fundamental diagrams. *Applied Soft Computing, 38*, 134–150.

Sugeno, M., & Kang, G. (1988). Structure identification of fuzzy model. *Fuzzy Sets and Systems, 28*, 15–33.

Tatomir, B., & Rothkrantz, L. (2006). Hierarchical routing in traffic using swarm-intelligence. In *2006 IEEE Intelligent Transportation Systems Conference* (pp. 230–235). IEEE.

Teodorović, D. (1994). Fuzzy sets theory applications in traffic and transportation. *European Journal of Operational Research, 74*, 379–390.

Teodorović, D. (2008). Swarm intelligence systems for transportation engineering: Principles and applications. *Transportation Research Part C: Emerging Technologies, 16*, 651–667.

Teodorović, D., & Lučić, P. (2005). Schedule synchronization in public transit using the fuzzy ant system. *Transportation Planning and Technology, 28*, 47–76.

Teodorović, D., & Lučić, P. (2007). The fuzzy ant system for the vehicle routing problem when demand at nodes is uncertain. *International Journal on Artificial Intelligence Tools, 16*, 751–770.

Yager, R. R. (1982). A new approach to the summarization of data. *Information Sciences, 28,* 69–86.

Zadeh, L. A. (1975). The concept of a linguistic variable and its application to approximate reasoning II. *Information Sciences, 8,* 301–357.

Zadeh, L. A. (1996). Soft computing and fuzzy logic. In *Fuzzy Sets, Fuzzy Logic, and Fuzzy Systems: Selected Papers by Lotfi a Zadeh* (pp. 796–804). World Scientific.

Zadeh, L. A., Klir, G. J., & Yuan, B. (1996). *Fuzzy sets, fuzzy logic, and fuzzy systems: selected papers* (Vol. 6). World Scientific.

Part III
Applications

Chapter 4
Fuzzifying Geospatial Traffic Data to Convey Information

4.1 Critical Traffic Areas Identification

This section presents the results of a fuzzy data-driven framework to identify areas that present traffic anomalies, using probe data from delivery vehicles with a low penetration rate and recorded traffic messages from a traffic information center. It is intended to address the complexities of generalizing traffic conditions from low sampling probe data derived from business operations and the imprecision and ambiguity that dealing with transportation parameters entails. Furthermore, this effort aims at providing an analysis tool for industrial practitioners.

4.1.1 Conceptual Development

There is no universal definition of traffic congestion. However, according to Aftabuzzaman (2007), the definitions found in literature can be categorized into three groups: (i) demand capacity related, meaning that traffic congestion occurs when travel demand exceeds the existing road capacity, (ii) delay-travel time related, which implies travel time or delay more than the generally incurred under free-flow travel conditions, and (iii) cost-related, which refers to the incremental costs resulting from interference among road users. Moreover, systematic road network-wide assessment is an essential indicator for decision-making in transportation, especially in the logistics and delivery domain.

Advanced travel information system research seeks to determine where and when traffic congestion occurs intending to reduce the time spent on the roads (Thiagarajan et al., 2011; Yuan et al., 2011). In the last few years, many studies have been directed to forecast vehicle speeds, traffic flows, transportation cost, and other traffic variables. Such initiatives are based on one-time series methods, simulations, nonparametric approaches, regression, and neural networks. All of them have in

© The Author(s), under exclusive license to Springer Nature Switzerland AG 2022
J. Pincay Nieves, *Smart Urban Logistics*, Fuzzy Management Methods,
https://doi.org/10.1007/978-3-031-16704-1_4

common the requirement of large amounts of precise information and, at times, constant tracking of the vehicles circulating on the roads and streets (Li et al., 2006; Pang et al., 2013).

One source of data to perform traffic analysis is the recorded by GPS devices fitted on vehicles. These data are known as floating car data and, when the records correspond to the movement of vehicles circulating for specific duties (e.g., taxis and logistic trucks), they are known as probe data (Chen et al., 2015; D'Andrea & Marcelloni, 2017; Pang et al., 2013). Significant insights such as route circulation patterns can be derived from probe data; however, there are some limitations of working with this type of data, including neglecting the dynamic changes over time of traffic conditions, incomplete and uncertain data, and how people perceive traffic. Furthermore, transportation and traffic parameters are defined in uncertain, imprecise, ambiguous, and subjective terms (Aftabuzzaman, 2007; Teodorović, 1994). Thus, methods that enable capturing and processing such characteristics are needed.

The concept of type-2 fuzzy sets, proposed by Zadeh (1975) and further studied by Mendel (2007), is a promising approach to deal with the ambiguity and incompleteness of traffic-related data due to its capacity of handling randomness and uncertainties in measurements (Li et al., 2006, 2016).

According to Pedrycz (2020), two considerations need to be taken into account to decide when to use T2 FS. Firstly, the need to apply them must be clear, and their use should be straightforward, and secondly, there is a sound membership definition procedure that grants the definition of the fuzzy sets. Pedrycz (2020) also proposes an example that illustrates how to deal with the considerations above; in the case of having several datasets coming from different regions that present the influence of locality, they likely have some variability. Through T2 FS, this variability can be better captured, and the result of the aggregation of the datasets can be more faithful to reality. These last statements support the author's decision of choosing IT2 FS (see Sect. 3.1.1.2) in the development of this work, provided that databases of different nature describing uncertain traffic-related data are used.

The next section provides an overview of how type-2 fuzzy sets have been applied in traffic modeling.

4.1.2 Type-2 Fuzzy Sets and Traffic Models

Several preceding initiatives that applied type-2 fuzzy sets in traffic-related topics are described in this section.

The authors Li et al. (2006) built a type-2 fuzzy logic forecasting model for short-term traffic prediction. Historical and real-time data were combined to generate a traffic forecast that was performed and other approaches reported in the literature. T2 FS performed well handling and including uncertainties derived from the traffic analysis. The main limitations of this work included the usage of interval fuzzy sets for the fuzzy engine and the simple average for the defuzzification process.

Another related initiative is the one of Nagarajan et al. (2019). The authors proposed a new perspective on traffic control management through the use of triangular IT2 FS and interval neutrosophic sets. The researchers concluded that the application of T2 FS enables the definition of rules that accept uncertainties completely, adaptiveness, and novelty. On the other hand, the computational complexity was larger than in other methods given that the membership functions describing the sets are fuzzy themselves.

In the work of Li et al. (2016), a long-term forecasting scheme based on IT2 FS was developed. The central limit theorem was applied to convert traffic flow point data into confidence intervals to obtain the membership functions for the T2 FS. The method developed by the researchers handled the uncertainty and randomness of traffic flow while diminishing the effects of noise from the data. It was found that the use of upper and lower limits to forecasting the results enables a higher prediction of traffic flow with high precision and stable errors.

Contrary to the prior efforts, this project proposes a framework to fuzzify probe data and traffic-related incidents to identify different types of critical traffic areas while addressing the issues of working with low penetration data and imprecision in traffic measurement. Moreover, this work seeks to develop an analysis tool that does not require large amounts of data and eases the interpretation of data from two very different data sources. The following sections are dedicated to explaining the design of such framework and instantiation.

4.1.3 Framework and Artifact Design

The design science research for information systems guidelines with a transdisciplinary approach was adopted to conduct this research work. The framework to identify critical traffic areas is built upon four main components: (i) data cleaner, (ii) fuzzifier, (iii) fuzzy inference engine, and (iv) visualizer. It takes inspiration from the IT2 FLS proposed by Mendel (2007) and the practical implementation completed by Li et al. (2006). Figure 4.1 depicts these components and their main operations.

4.1.3.1 Data Cleaner

Before presenting details about the data sources and the cleaning process used in the development, the concept of geospatial indexing and Geohash is explained.

Geospatial Indexing—Geohash
In a dictionary, an index facilitates localizing an entry in the vast list of words. Following this idea, database systems introduced the concept of indexing to improve the retrieval of records when performing queries.

Fig. 4.1 Framework to identify critical traffic areas based on type-2 fuzzy sets. Adapted from Pincay et al. (2021a)

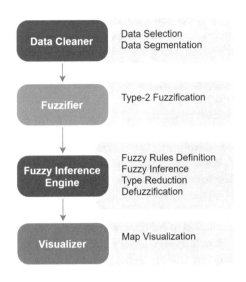

Geospatial data, also known as spatial data, refer to geographical information such as longitudes and latitudes alongside other non-spatial information. Geospatial indexes are likewise data structures developed for efficient handling, storage and retrieval, and geospatial data processing. Some examples of operations they support include retrieving data points within a specific geographical area or finding similar points within a specific space interval. The geospatial indexes are usually implemented from well-known basic indexing structures such as sorted arrays, binary trees, B-trees, quadtrees, and hashing (Lu & Ooi, 1993).

Geohash (or geohashing) is one example of a geospatial index. Geohash is a hierarchical spatial data structure based on the Z-order curve. A Z-order curve is a space-filling curve that iterates through space in a Z manner. Geohashing iteratively subdivides space into grid buckets or bounding boxes, producing different precision at various hierarchies (Vukovic, 2016). In practice, this means that several geographic coordinates are mapped to a single bounding box, which has a unique identifier that serves as an index to retrieve specific coordinates. The number of coordinates associated with a bounding box depends on the level of granularity (i.e., the bigger the bounding box, the larger the number of geographic coordinates contained). Figure 4.2 illustrates the hierarchical and granular nature of the geohash indexing approach at three levels; a unique string is assigned to bounding boxes encompassing geographical spaces. Further iterations of the geohash algorithm increase the precision of bounding boxes and, correspondingly, the length of the string identifier. Table 4.1 presents the geohash precision levels and their corresponding bounding boxes size.

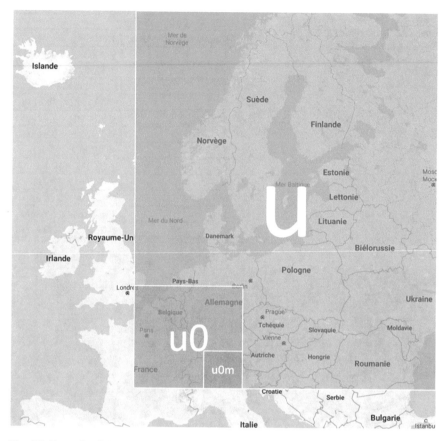

Fig. 4.2 Example of the geohash hierarchical geospatial data structure at 3 levels. Adapted from Pincay et al. (2020a)

One implementation of geohashing is available on geohash.org.[1] This service allows mapping geographical coordinates to a $(0 - z)$ unique hash of 32 bits. For example, the point $x = (46.8045, 7.169)$ is converted to the geohash value of $u0m470$. One key feature of geohash is that the length of the geohash describes the precision level. Removing bits from the tail of the geohash decreases point precision while not changing its position in space (Vukovic, 2016). This property is convenient in cases when performance is more important than precision. For the previous example, the point x is mapped to the geohash $u0m470$ at level 6 and to the geohash $u0m470k$ at level 7. Note that only one character (k) has been added to the existing geohash code.

---

[1] http://geohash.org.

Table 4.1 Geohash precision levels and their respective bounding boxes (bbox) as presented in Pincay et al. (2020a)

Geohash spatial indexing	
Geohash precision level	Bounding box area
1	$\leq 5000\,km \times 5000\,km$
2	$\leq 1250\,km \times 1250\,km$
3	$\leq 156\,km \times 156\,km$
4	$\leq 39.1\,km \times 19.5\,km$
5	$\leq 4.89\,km \times 4.89\,km$
6	$\leq 1.22\,km \times 0.61\,km$
7	$\leq 153\,m \times 153\,m$
8	$\leq 38.2\,m \times 19.1\,m$
9	$\leq 4.77\,m \times 4.77\,m$
10	$\leq 1.19\,m \times 0.59\,m$
11	$\leq 149\,mm \times 149\,mm$
12	$\leq 37.2\,mm \times 18.6\,mm$

Fig. 4.3 The point $x = (46.8045, 7.169)$ mapped to geohash codes in levels 6 (left) and 7 (right). Adapted from Pincay et al. (2020a)

As an example, Fig. 4.3 illustrates the effect of going from level 6 to 7 for the aforementioned coordinates. Strings derived from the encoding, named geohashes, preserve local proximity to other geohashes. Unlike other geospatial index structures, geohash provides a straightforward approach for granularity analysis and the reduction of spatial coordinates for pattern discovery without multiple preprocessing (La Valley et al., 2017).

Geohash, therefore, provides the means of specifying a spatial interval for dividing a road trajectory into segments and hence is used for the segmentation followed in this research work.

Data Sources
Two different data sources were used in the development of the case study:

1. DBT_1—*Probe data:* GPS data of 6 months of operations of logistic vehicles of *Swiss Post*. Its records contained information on the location of the vehicles during their delivery operations, among them are mileage, speed, events (e.g., parked, motor on, and motor off), and postal code. Only data points of the area of Bern (Switzerland) were considered. The operations performed on the dataset included the following:

   (a) Duplicates and inconsistent and invalid records were removed.
   (b) Selection of records timestamped from 6 A.M. to 10 A.M.
   (c) Segmentation through level 7 geohashes[2] to perform an average speed deduction on a segment fashion. Moreover, the geohashes are later used for visualization.

2. DBT_2—*Traffic Message Channel-based records:* The second data source consisted of traffic messages delivered through the Traffic Message Channel (TMC) technology (Gao & Wen, 2007) and processed by *Viasuisse*, the Swiss national competence center for traffic, during the years 2018–2020. These messages are generated by the traffic monitoring responsible (i.e., police officers and municipalities), and they record incidents varying from traffic anomalies and road accidents to road works and events that might cause traffic delays. The following steps were followed when selecting the data:

   (a) Messages containing on their description these words (translated from German) were selected: *traffic, stagnant, heavy traffic, lost time, waiting time, traffic suspended until further notice,* and *traffic obstruction.*
   (b) Duplicates and inconsistent and invalid records were removed. Records timestamped from 6 A.M. to 10 A.M. were selected.
   (c) Given that the records contained only the start and end locations where the traffic incident occurs, the locations between the start and end were augmented onto the database, as these locations are also affected by the traffic anomaly. To this end, the official Swiss TMC location code table provided by *Viasuisse* was used.
   (d) The duration in minutes of the traffic incidents was deduced according to the rules explained during workshops accomplished during the development of this project.
   (e) GPS coordinates of the locations registering anomalies were converted to level 7 geohashes, to be used later for aggregation and visualization purposes.

Moreover, the information recorded on the DBT_1 consisted of geospatial information located mainly on the streets of Bern; the data register on DBT_2 contained information of traffic events that happened on the main highways surrounding Bern and the principal axes that go through the city.

---

[2] https://www.movable-type.co.uk/scripts/geohash.html.

4.1.3.2 Fuzzifier

Once the data sources have been cleaned, it is necessary to select the variables of interest. From the DBT_1, the deduced speed ss at the different segments was selected, and from the DBT_2, the time of traffic anomalies tt recorded was the explicit variable to be observed. The input variables are crisp values. Thus, the fuzzifier is in charge of taking those crisp values to fuzzy ones. To that effect, the parametric principle of justifiable granularity to build type-2 membership functions was applied (Pedrycz & Wang, 2015). By implementing this principle, it is ensured that the membership functions are built so that they are experimentally justifiable and exhibit sound semantics.

Moreover, given the nature of the data and as per the guidelines of the principle of justifiable granularity, the datasets were split using clustering (Pedrycz, 2020; Pedrycz & Wang, 2015), and their centroids were used as prototypes of each set; later, the principle is applied to the individual subsets. The resulting membership functions used in this work are Gaussian with fixed standard deviation σ and uncertain mean m, considering that the mean traffic time over the time, as well as the mean speed with what vehicle circulates, is uncertain, and it was desired to capture that variability when adjusting the membership functions. The following expression defines the membership functions for our two variables.

$$A(x; m, \sigma) = e^{-\frac{1}{2}(\frac{x-m}{\sigma})^2} \quad m \in [m_1, m_2] \tag{4.1}$$

being the interval m_1, m_2 defined over the historical data. As type-2 fuzzy sets are defined, the upper and lower membership functions need to be defined as well. The upper membership function is given by

$$\bar{\mu}_{\tilde{A}(x)} = \begin{cases} A(x; m_1, \sigma) & x \le m_1 \\ 1 & m_1 \le x \le m_2 \\ A(x; m_2, \sigma) & x \ge m_2 \end{cases} \tag{4.2}$$

And the lower membership function is defined by

$$\underline{\mu}_{\tilde{A}(x)} = \begin{cases} A(x; m2, \sigma) \ x \le \frac{m_1+m_2}{2} \\ A(x; m1, \sigma) \ x \ge \frac{m_1+m_2}{2} \end{cases} \tag{4.3}$$

4.1.3.3 Fuzzy Inference Engine

As defined by Mendel (2007), rules are the core of a fuzzy logic system, and in this case, they were defined from the available data.

The fuzzy rules handle the fuzzy values input coming from the definitions of the type-2 fuzzy sets. They are declared as a set of IF-THEN clauses, with the IF-part being the antecedent and the THEN-portion the consequent. The ith rule of the fuzzy engine has the following format:

IF ss is F_e^1 and tt is F_e^2 THEN tc is G_e^1

where F_i^l is the antecedent, G_e^n is the consequent, ss is the input variable that corresponds to the *segment speed*, tt is the *traffic time*, and (tc is the output, which describes the *traffic criticality*, meaning how critical is the traffic in a determined zone.

Moreover, the fuzzy inferential engine calculates a so-called *firing level* for each of the rules defined, based on the input and antecedents of the rules; the firing level is then applied to shape the consequent fuzzy sets. The inferential engine implemented in this works follows an interval type-2 Mamdani fuzzy logic system, which uses minimum and product implication models (Mendel, 2007).

Given that the consequent will be mapped into a type-2 set, a *type reduction* to type-1 one fuzzy set and a *defuzzification* process needs to be conducted as well to obtain a crisp output. These two steps need to be executed to use the output later and visualize a score on a map. To this end, the Karnik–Mendel (KM) algorithms with center-of-sets defuzzification are used as they are easy to use and implement, and they converge to the solutions monotonically and super-exponentially fast (Karnik & Mendel, 2001; Mendel, 2007). After the type reduction takes place, an interval set $[y_l(x), y_r(x)]$ is obtained; the final defuzzified value is computed by averaging $[y_l(x)$ and $y_r(x)]$. Figure 4.4 presents a summary of the computations performed in this stage.

4.1.3.4 Visualizer

The visualizer allows displaying how critical, in terms of traffic, a zone is (output (tc) of the IT2 FLS). For that effect, the historical values of speed and recorded traffic time per geohash segment are fed to the IT2 FLS. The output results are then aggregated and visualized on a map.

4.1.4 Implementation and Results

The implementation results of the artifact built upon the methods explained in Sect. 4.1.3 are presented next.

The `Python` programming language was used to perform the data cleaning, and the package `pyit2fls` (Haghrah & Ghaemi, 2019) was used to fuzzify the data and the library `Folium` for the visualization. A code sample of the definition of the fuzzy sets and the inference data is presented in Appendix B.

After the data cleaning process, the DBT_1 was composed of about 315,014 sampling points, and each record was described in terms of 14 fields among which there were position, timestamps, distance, non-traffic vehicular related information,

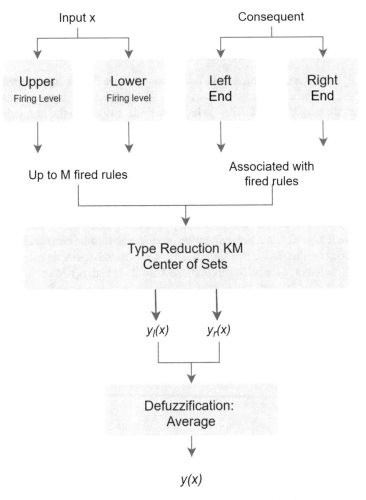

Fig. 4.4 Computations of the Fuzzy Inference Engine, adapted from Mendel (2007)

and events depicting internal vehicular state such as power on/off, ignition, movement, and waiting. Once the selection, segmentation, and calculation of the segment speed were made, the final database had 34,470 records which contained timestamp information, deduced speed, and the GPS coordinates encoded with geohash.

Regarding the DBT_2, once the cleaning and selection steps were completed, it was formed by 3008 records and 15 fields. Some of they are timestamps of the start and end of the event, coordinates and names of the start and end locations, duration, and description of the event. Furthermore, after the data augmentation process took place, the total records in the database were 5013. These final records contained additional fields depicting the time of the day and the coordinates where the incident happened encoded with geohash.

4.1.4.1 Fuzzification and Inference

With the data selection, it was possible to define the type-2 fuzzy sets for the selected variables. As it was previously defined, the principle of justifiable granularity was applied over both datasets, using the programming language Python and the library `pyit2fls`.

Figure 4.5 (top) presents the IT2 FS for the variable segment speed ss obtained from the DBT_1; the values on the horizontal axis correspond to the speed in KM/H, which has been scaled (1 : 100) for visualization and processing purposes. Figure 4.5 (bottom) shows the resulting IT2 FS for the variable traffic time, derived from the DBT_2; the values on the horizontal scale correspond to the duration of a traffic anomaly in minutes, which have scaled (1 : 100) as well, for visualization and processing purposes.

The implementation of the fuzzy system took place afterward. It started with the definition of the fuzzy rules. A total of sixteen rules could be obtained from the combination of the two observed variables. Table 4.2 shows four of the rules that were used in the implementation of the IT2 FLS. Furthermore, as previously described, the IT2 FLS follows the Mamdani model that was also implemented using the `pyit2fls` package.

The output domain is defined in the interval [0, 1] for simplicity, with Gaussian membership functions with uncertain mean, similar to how the input sets were defined. Figure 4.6 depicts the output set of the IT2 FLS indicating the traffic criticality tc.

As an example of output, consider the value of the segment speed $ss = 0.45$ meaning *low speed* and the traffic time $tt = 0.49$ meaning *medium traffic time*; after running the IT2 FLS, the result for the traffic criticality is $tc = 0.67$, which indicates that the area presenting such characteristics is a *critical* one. Figure 4.7 presents the results of the output tc for the aforementioned input with the type-2 result and the reduced one.

4.1.4.2 Verification of the Design Criteria for Fuzzy Sets

As it was presented in Sect. 3.1.5.2, some certain criteria and constraints need to be followed to guarantee that the defined fuzzy sets depict reality adequately. Such criteria were verified for the fuzzy sets that were previously defined: segment speed (ss), traffic time (tt), and traffic criticality (tc).

The criteria of normality, continuity, and convexity are met since each function has at least a prototype, they are continuous, and even when the fuzzy sets in question are type-2, it can be observed that the membership values within the intervals are not lower than the ones of the extremes. Moreover, the design constraints for the definition of the linguistic variables are also met. Special attention was given to the constraint leftmost/rightmost fuzzy sets and distinguishability since, in this case, type-2 fuzzy sets were used and the overlapping between them needs to be carefully examined.

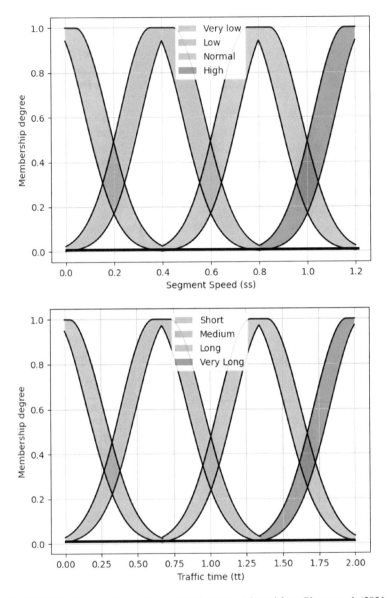

Fig. 4.5 IT2 FS for the variables *ss* (top) and *tt* (bottom). Adapted from Pincay et al. (2021a)

4.1.4.3   Visualization

The visualization of the traffic criticality was performed using the crisp output of
the IT2 FLS and implemented with Python, using the libraries `Folium` to render

Table 4.2 Sample of the fuzzy IF-THEN rules base of the IT2 FLS. Adapted from Pincay et al. (2021a)

	Antecedent		Consequent
Rule	*ss*	*tt*	*tc*
R1	High	Short	Not critical
R2	Normal	Medium	Low critical
R3	Low	Long	Critical
R4	Very low	Very long	Very critical

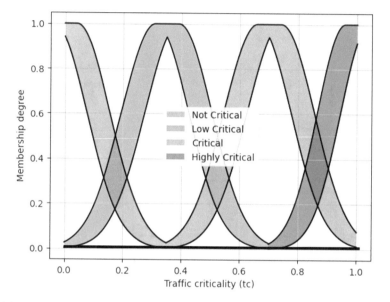

Fig. 4.6 Output type-2 fuzzy set depicting traffic criticality *tc*. Adapted from Pincay et al. (2021a)

the maps and `Libgeohash`[3] to handle the geohash encoding of the locations. Figure 4.8 shows an example of the visualization for two areas in the surroundings of Bern. It should be indicated that the data displayed correspond to records timestamped in the morning, between 6 A.M. and 10 A.M.

4.1.5 Summary and Lessons Learned

This project introduced a framework to enable the design of an artifact to analyze criticality of traffic zones. Powered by type-2 fuzzy sets, this endeavor aimed at capturing and handling the uncertainty, incompleteness, and randomness of traffic-related data to represent reality more faithfully.

---

[3] https://pypi.org/project/libgeohash/.

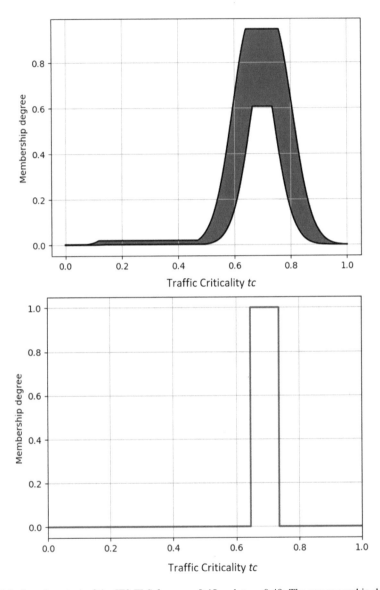

Fig. 4.7 Sample output of the IT2 FLS for $ss = 0.45$ and $tt = 0.49$. The upper graphic denotes the type-2 result and the lower the type-reduced one. Adapted from Pincay et al. (2021a)

The proposed framework has four main components: (i) data cleaner, (ii) fuzzifier, (iii) fuzzy inference engine, and (iv) visualizer. The data clear executes processes for selecting data and deducing speed values from probe data and traffic time duration from TMC-based messages. The fuzzifier applies the principle of parametric justifiable granularity to convert the crisp input data into type-2 fuzzy

Fig. 4.8 Example of the visualization results from Pincay et al. (2021a)

sets, with Gaussian membership functions with uncertain mean. After defining fuzzy rules, the fuzzy inference engine performs an inference, followed by a type reduction and defuzzification to produce an output score. This output represents the traffic criticality of a geographic area. Lastly, the scores obtained from the fuzzy inference engine are aggregated and visualized on a map.

Despite the existing efforts, this framework distinguishes itself for its praxis-oriented nature, transdisciplinarity, and the type of data used in its implementation. The practice knowledge derived from this work is also valuable; it enabled to get insights from the data sources that would have been impossible to obtain by themselves. Also, it was possible to provide guidelines for the development of future tools that follow digital ethics and privacy principles. This last statement is claimed since no data resulting from the constant tracking of non-aware users were used, yet significant results were obtained.

The outcome of this effort was discussed with the practice partners. As per their knowledge and by comparing the obtained insights to their existing running systems, the results showed consistency and helped confirm several conjectures they already had and raised awareness of several aspects that were being overlooked.

Furthermore, this research project contributed with a practical implementation that uses fuzzy sets of higher order. Thus, it also contributes to the assessment of how approximate methods (i.e., fuzzy logic and computational intelligence) could be applied to develop working solutions that do not need large amounts of precise information (i.e., machine learning solutions) and that can combine data of different nature to give them a new meaning. The results obtained in this effort could be used to develop other solutions in the field of green logistics, urban planning, and traffic control.

Future work will be directed toward determining if T2 FS are effective in handling the uncertainty of data of larger regions. Having large dispersion of data among regions might imply broader FOUs, and, in that case, a more appropriate solution could be having two (or more) different inference systems where the parameters are adjusted to the regional characteristics as suggested by Mináriková (2021).

4.2 Linguistic Summarization of Traffic Data

This section provides details of the development and results of an artifact whose goal is to obtain Linguistic Summary (LS) from two databases that contain data related to traffic incidents and their duration. Through the development of the project and with a trandisciplinary approach, it was intended to provide notions about how to integrate heterogeneous traffic data and convey information to users who do not necessarily have a comprehensive understanding of traffic analysis.

4.2.1 Conceptual Development

Human-Smart Cities aim to enhance the city services to improve the quality of life and inclusion of people living or working there. Informing citizens and stakeholders is thus a crucial aspect toward developing solutions that answer to the needs of the people (Colombo et al., 2020a,b). However, the large amounts of daily data bring challenges when communicating to an audience who does not necessarily have technical knowledge but needs to be informed.

Linguistic summaries allow verbalizing information by quantified sentences and are an alternative to address the issue above. They are based on the fuzzy set theory, and thus, adjectives and adverbs can be used more thoroughly when verbalizing information (Hudec, 2019; Zadeh et al., 1996). For instance, the sentence *about half of young citizens have a high interest in traffic topics* could be easier to understand than providing figures and numbers.

Traffic-related data can be challenging to examine and understand given their heterogeneity and volume (Pincay et al., 2020b). Moreover, transportation and traffic parameters are defined in uncertain, imprecise, ambiguous, and subjective terms (Aftabuzzaman, 2007; Pincay et al., 2020). At the same time, traffic-related information is of interest to the vast majority of people using the roads for transportation.

Linguistic summaries are a suitable option for providing compact but valuable descriptions of the data. Certainly, LSs might not provide a clear image of a specific situation, but they can be a valuable tool to explain problems and behaviors and make, for instance, more citizens participate in the development of smart solutions.

4.2.2 Linguistic Summaries for Traffic

Alvarez-Alvarez et al. (2012) designed an application that generates linguistic descriptions of evolving traffic behavior to assist traffic managers in decision-making tasks. To this effect, the researchers applied concepts of computing with words and fuzzy rules to extract summaries from actual and simulated traffic reports. The approach was validated by generating linguistic descriptions from input data derived through image processing techniques from a video stream. The authors found that it was possible to obtain various linguistic reports customized to the users' needs.

In the work of Trivino et al. (2010), the details about the implementation of a system that generates sentences to describe traffic perceptions in natural language were presented. Through computer vision techniques, features from traffic images of a roundabout were extracted; these features were the input of a linguistic model capable of spawning text descriptions of the observed phenomena. Fuzzy logic techniques were then used to compute the validity of the linguistic descriptions. As per the experimental results of the study, it was found that the text descriptions produced by the system were comparable to the descriptions that a human being could provide. However, the researchers also manifested that their implementation needed further tuning.

Another relative initiative is the research effort of Popek et al. (2011). The authors provided an overview of a distributed agent-based system that delivers summaries of city traffic in a textual form. Their system could deal with incomplete data collected through traffic sensors and provide descriptions of traffic states with auto-epistemic operators of possibility, belief, and knowledge. The summaries generated by each agent were then aggregated to provide summaries for a region.

Contrary to the previous related work, this initiative pretends to ease understanding heterogeneous traffic data to everyday users. Following a transdisciplinary approach and implementing an artifact that spawns meaningful linguistic summaries, it is expected to provide notions to researchers on how applying fuzzy methods to large and diverse datasets enables helping people to convey information quickly and effectively.

The following sections are devoted to describing the design of such artifact and its instantiation.

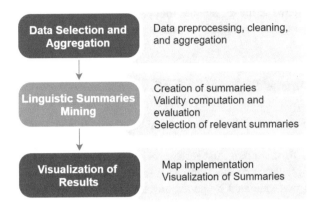

Fig. 4.9 Method followed in the development of the LSs artifact. Adapted from Pincay et al. (2021b)

4.2.3   Framework and Artifact Design

In a similar manner as the application described in Sect. 4.1, this effort was conducted following the guidelines of the design science research for information systems in conjunction with a transdisciplinary approach. The development consisted of three main stages: (i) data selection and aggregation, (ii) linguistic summaries mining, and (iii) visualization of results.

Figure 4.9 outlines the method followed in the artifact design and the main steps conducted in each stage.

4.2.3.1   Data Selection and Aggregation

Two data sources were used in the development of the artifact:

1. $DBLS_1$—*Traffic Message Channel-based records:* The first data source is formed by traffic messages delivered through the TMC technology (Gao & Wen, 2007) and processed by *Viasuisse* during 2020. Such messages record various incidents that may cause traffic anomalies (e.g., traffic congestion, accidents, road works, and events), and they are reported to the competence center for traffic by traffic monitoring responsible (e.g., road police and municipalities).

   Given the large number of recorded messages, the following steps were conducted to select the records of interest.

   (a) Entries whose description included the following words (translated from German) were selected: *traffic, stagnant, heavy traffic, lost time, waiting time*, and *speed is limited*.
   (b) Events that lasted more than 1 day (e.g., constructions on the road) were neglected.

(c) Only events that took place on the main highways of Switzerland[4] were considered (i.e., A1–A9, A12–A14, A16, A18, A21, A22, and A40).

(d) The reasons for the traffic anomalies were also deducted from the text descriptions. The reasons of interest of *Viasuisse* were *construction site, accident, fire, storm,* and *overload.*

(e) The duration in hours of the traffic anomalies was computed according to the guidelines provided by the data partner.

2. *DBLS$_2$—Traffic Criticality Score:* This is a database derived from a IT2 FS. This system uses TMC messages and GPS floating data to provide a score between 0 and 1; this score depicts the traffic criticality of zones (i.e., not critical, low critical, critical, and highly critical) that belong to the city of Bern. This data source was the result of the application presented in Sect. 4.1. The whole available database was used for this project.

4.2.3.2   Linguistic Summaries Mining

According to Maybury (1999), summarization consists of determining the most relevant parts of information from a source to produce a version of it that is of interest to a user. In this research effort, the linguistic summaries were created following a data-driven approach. This means that summaries were generated according to a set of predefined quantifiers and predicates and selected according to their validity.

The linguistic summaries research task is defined as (Hudec, 2016; Liu, 2011):

$$find \ \ Q, S, R$$

$$subject \ \ to$$

$$Q \in \bar{Q}, \ R \in \bar{R}, \ S \in \bar{S}, \ v(Q, S, R) \geq \beta \qquad (4.4)$$

where $\bar{Q}$ is a set of quantifiers of interest, $\bar{R}$ and $\bar{S}$ are sets of relevant linguistic expressions for restriction and summarizer respectively, and β is threshold value from the (0, 1] interval. Each of the possible solutions creates a linguistic summary of the form (Q^*, R^* are S^*).

For the $DBLS_1$, the objective was to unveil all relevant LSs throughout all the traffic incidents. The quantifier set $\bar{Q}$ was defined with the linguistic terms *few, about half,* and *most.* On the other hand, the summarizers of the normalized duration in hours $\bar{S}$ were *short, medium, long,* and *very long.*

---

[4] https://www.astra.admin.ch/astra/de/home/themen/nationalstrassen/nationalstrassennetz/neb.html.

For the sake of this work, the linguistic expressions for restriction $\bar{R}$ were not taken into consideration as they did not add value. Figure 4.10 presents a plot of the quantifiers and summarizers used to mine the LSs from $DBLS_1$.

For $DBLS_2$, the same quantifier as the previous case was used. For the traffic criticality score, the terms set of summarizers $\bar{S}$ were *not critical, low critical, critical*, and *highly critical*. Figure 4.11 depicts the plot of summarizers used to mine the LSs from the $DBLS_2$.

Furthermore, all LSs resulting from the combination of the quantifiers and summarizers were generated, and their validity was computed (see Eq. 3.6). Ultimately, only the summaries with validity greater than or equal to 0.6 ($\beta \geq 0.6$) were considered as relevant and therefore selected. The value of 0.6 was chosen given the results obtained from the data and after consultation with the data partners about how the traffic incidents occur, based on their experience.

4.2.3.3 Visualization of Results

Maps were generated using the geospatial information of $DBLS_1$ and $DBLS_2$. The most relevant summaries accompanied the maps besides the absolute numbers of the traffic anomalies duration and criticality score.

The maps and the summaries were later used to perform evaluations with users. The resulting visualizations are presented in Sect. 4.2.5.

4.2.4 Implementation and Results

The Python programming language was used to perform the data selection, and the framework Django was used to build a functional web application to display the maps and the summaries to the users. The library Simpful (Spolaor et al., 2020), a Python library for fuzzy logic reasoning, was used to define the linguistic variables for the quantifiers $\bar{Q}$ and summarizers $\bar{S}$ and to perform the evaluations over the data. Finally, the library Folium was used to create the maps.

After the data selection and aggregation process was completed, the $DBLS_1$ had 687,644 sampling records. Each of the records was described in terms of 15 fields, among which there were timestamps of the start and end of the event, geographical coordinates and names of the start and end locations, duration, description of the event, and the cause of the traffic anomaly.

On the other hand, the $DBLS_2$ had 67,643 records, and their fields contained the GPS coordinates of the zones with information available, timestamps, and criticality scores.

Moreover, the data of $DBLS_1$ and $DBLS_2$ were integrated into a single PostgreSQL database to make it available to the Django web application.

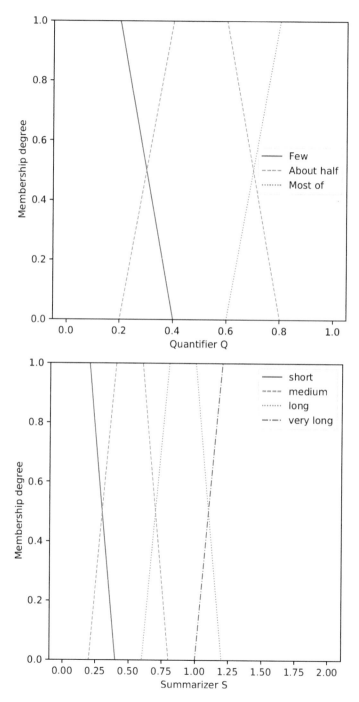

Fig. 4.10 Plot of the term sets for the quantifiers and summarizers of $DBLS_1$. Adapted from Pincay et al. (2021b)

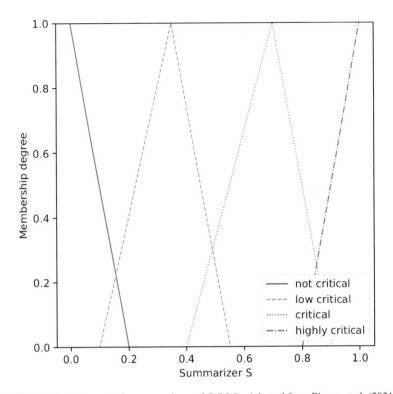

Fig. 4.11 Plot of the term sets for summarizers of $DBLS_2$. Adapted from Pincay et al. (2021b)

4.2.4.1 Linguistic Summaries Mining

Through the functions of the library Simpful, the linguistic values depicting the quantifiers and summarizers defined in Sect. 4.2.3.2 were implemented in Python. Furthermore, the validity of all the potential summaries (i.e., a combination of all summarizers and quantifiers) was computed to discover the relevant ones.

This process was executed for $DBLS_1$ and $DBLS_2$. Table 4.3 presents the validity results for all possible LSs that could be obtained from the duration of all traffic anomalies existing in $DBLS_1$; however, only the ones in bold (i.e., with validity greater than or equal to 0.6) are relevant and thus were the ones that describe the database properly.

Moreover, given that $DBLS_1$ contained information at finer granularity (i.e., causes of the traffic incident and name of the highways), further summaries were mined. For instance, for the highway $A12$, the following summaries were obtained:

- *Few of the incidents were caused by road works*, validity: 1.
- *Most of the incidents were caused by congestion*, validity: 0.64.
- *Few of the incidents were caused by accidents*, validity: 0.63.

Table 4.3 Validity values of LSs created from the linguistic term sets from the duration of all traffic incidents of $DBLS_1$. Adapted from Pincay et al. (2021b)

Linguistic summary	$v(Qx(P(x)))$
Few of the incidents had a short duration	0
Few of the incidents had a medium duration	0.19
Few of the incidents had a long duration	0.45
Few of the incidents had a very long duration	**0.75**
About half of the incidents had a short duration	**0.72**
About half of the incidents had a medium duration	0.43
About half of the incidents had a long duration	0.37
About half of the incidents had a very long duration	0.25
Most of the incidents had a short duration	0
Most of the incidents had a medium duration	0
Most of the incidents had a long duration	0
Most of the incidents had a very long duration	0

For the entire $DBLS_2$, four valid summaries were obtained. For instance, one of them was *Few of the traffic zones are highly critical*, which had a validity of 0.9346. Moreover, given that this database was smaller than $DBLS_1$ and that it only covered the city of Bern, it was decided to split the dataset by dayparts (i.e., morning, midday, afternoon, evening, and night) and mine LSs from each subset. However, the valid summaries were almost the same for each daypart.

4.2.4.2   Verification of the Design Criteria for Linguistic Variables

As it was explained in Sect. 3.1.5, when dealing with natural language expressions, it is imperative to keep the linguistic variables meaningful to the people. Thus, the linguistic variables defined for the quantifiers and summarizers presented in the previous section were validated against the design criteria for linguistic variables.

All criteria are met, and special attention was given to the constraint relation preservation since in this case it is crucial to keep a proper ordering of the concepts depicted. For the quantifiers, for example, they are $Q = few, about\ half, most\ of$ and they respect an ascending order of the meaning; another order will result in a wrong depiction of the summaries.

4.2.5   Visualization of Results

Map visualizations with the data of both databases and the valid linguistic summaries were created.

Through a web application, the users could visualize the total amount of traffic hours over the year 2020 and the places where more anomalies occurred. Moreover,

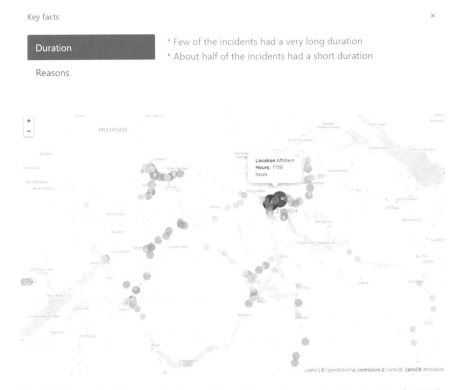

Fig. 4.12 Example of the visualization results and linguistic summaries for the data of $DBLS_1$. The color of the circles depicts the total time of the traffic events and the size of the number of records on the specific location. Taken from Pincay et al. (2021b)

the users were able to visualize all the highways' results or show results given a previous selection. It was also possible for the users to filter the results by the cause of the incident.

For the $DBLS_1$, two interfaces were created. The first one displays the summary of the total hours together with a map, and the second one shows *Key facts* which correspond to the mined linguistic summarizations. Figure 4.12 shows an example of the visualization presented to the user; in the upper part, the valid summaries for the whole network are presented as *Key facts* and in the lower part the map with the zones where there are traffic anomalies; the color of the circles depicts the total time of the traffic events and the size of the number of records on the specific location.

Additionally, both interfaces were later used to evaluate the perceived utility of the linguistic summaries (see Sect. 4.2.6).

A similar process was implemented for the data of the $DBLS_2$. However, only one interface was implemented as the data were different, and it represented a more abstract concept than traffic anomalies duration. Figure 4.13 depicts an example of the way the data of this database were displayed. For this case, a heatmap depicting

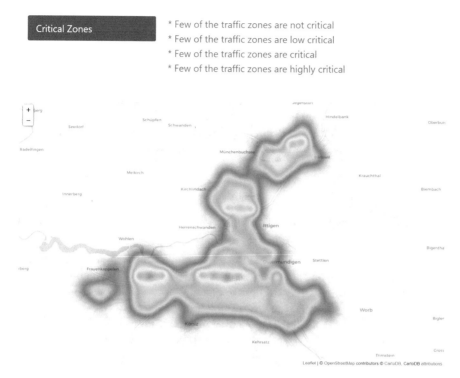

Fig. 4.13 Example of the visualization results and linguistic summaries for the data of $DBLS_2$. The orange color depicts areas with high traffic criticality, whereas the low traffic criticality areas are colored in green. Taken from Pincay et al. (2021b)

the areas with higher criticality was implemented. Moreover, users were able to select the daypart from where they wanted to observe the critical areas.

4.2.6   User's Evaluation

A survey was conducted to validate how valuable users with no experience in traffic analysis find the mined summaries.

Twenty people aged between 25 and 60 years old, 60% male and 40% female, answered the survey. Among them, 72% had some interest or were interested in traffic information and facts. Moreover, 95% of them considered that they had no experience with traffic data analysis.

The respondents were asked to observe the visualizations for the data of $DBLS_1$ and $DBLS_2$ with and without the summaries. Around 63% of the people manifested that having the *key facts* or summaries helped them to understand what the map was about in the case of the data of DB_1. For the visualization of the DB_2, 90% found the summaries helpful to understand the map. However, 72% manifested that the concept of traffic criticality was not clear enough, and a similar number specified that these summaries were not informative enough. Moreover, around 82% of the respondents answered that having the summaries contributed to understanding the data displayed in a more straightforward fashion.

Despite the encouraging results, around 60% of the respondents manifested that the summaries were essential and could be more informative if they were more detailed. This led to infer that the obtained summaries were perceived as practical but not enough to provide the users a comprehensive explanation of the information provided.

4.2.7 Summary and Lessons Learned

This research effort presented the results of the implementation of an artifact that sought to ease the understanding of heterogeneous traffic data. By mining linguistic summaries, this endeavor aimed to provide straightforward descriptions of traffic anomalies' duration and events to inform citizens more effectively.

Three main stages constituted the method that guided this development: (i) data selection and aggregation, (ii) linguistic summaries mining, and (iii) visualization of results. The data selection and aggregation allowed to obtain the subset of messages of interest coming from a TMC system and to obtain the duration in hours over the year 2020 of the events related to traffic anomalies of the main highways of Switzerland. Moreover, a dataset that scores the traffic criticality of different locations of the city of Bern was also used. The linguistic summaries mining process enabled identifying and validating summaries obtained from the data. With the visualization of results, it was possible to present to users map visualizations of the databases alongside *key facts* or summaries obtained from the data to facilitate the comprehension of the information provided.

The visualizations and summaries were implemented through a Python-based web application, and several users evaluated the perceived usefulness of the summaries provided. It was found that the summaries were perceived as helpful to understand the information seamlessly but that they were not detailed enough to have a deep understanding of the data.

Furthermore, special attention should be given to the validation process of the summaries. Given that the goal of using LSs is to convey meaningful information, the LSs need to be meaningful themselves. Moreover, the mining process has to be optimized from the implementation perspective since evaluating and aggregating large databases require considerable computation power. Furthermore, LSs can also be considered as a convenient alternative when it comes to exchanging data that could be sensitive.

Despite the related work, this research efforts project distinguishes itself given its praxis-oriented nature, transdisciplinarity, and real-life data used in the implementation. Furthermore, this initiative contributes with methods that enable making information more comprehensive to all citizens and not only to those with technical knowledge. The results obtained in this work can be further used as a basis to develop solutions in green logistics, urban planning, and traffic control.

4.3 Final Remarks

In this chapter, the development and results of two traffic-related projects were presented. The first project had as an outcome an artifact to analyze traffic criticality of geographical zones using probe data and TMC-based messages. The second endeavor aimed at understanding traffic facts in a straightforward manner from relatively complex databases.

From the first artifact, it was possible to learn how applying fuzzy methods the variability of traffic measurements can be better represented and captured to convey knowledge. Furthermore, it was possible to leverage the data of two heterogeneous data sources in the form of a *traffic score* that enabled ways of uncovering information that otherwise was not evident.

Given that such a traffic score can be difficult to understand for common users, the second artifact attempted to use linguistic summarizations to act as a bridge from technical information to a more understandable way of what is happening on the roads and streets.

Both approaches were presented in this chapter as an illustration of how fuzzy methods can be applied and extended to perform analysis and report to technical and non-technical audiences. Such capabilities could be still leveraged to develop more comprehensive solutions. Aiming to illustrate that, the concepts and results obtained in the development of these two projects are applied in the development of a framework to improve the first try of the last-mile delivery described in detail in Chap. 6.

4.4 Further Readings

- **Mendel (2007)** "This paper provides an introduction to and an overview of type-2 fuzzy sets and systems. It does this by answering the following questions: What is a T2 FS and how is it different from a T1 FS? Is there new terminology for a T2 FS? Are there important representations of a T2 FS and, if so, why are they important? How and why are T2 FSs used in a rule-based system?" (abs.).
- **Pedrycz and Wang (2015)** "This study is concerned with a design of membership functions of fuzzy sets. The membership functions are formed in such a way that they are experimentally justifiable and exhibit a sound semantics. These two requirements are articulated through the principle of justifiable granularity" (abs.).

- **Hudec (2016)** "This book explains the application of fuzzy approaches for classical relational databases and information systems, details important application aspects like fuzzy queries, fuzzy inference, and linguistic summaries, and includes a brief introduction to fuzzy sets and fuzzy logic" (abs.).

References

Aftabuzzaman, M. (2007). Measuring traffic congestion-a critical review. In *30th Australasian transport research forum* (1–16).

Alvarez-Alvarez, A., Sanchez-Valdes, D., Trivino, G., Sánchez, Á., & Suárez, P. D. (2012). Automatic linguistic report of traffic evolution in roads. *Expert Systems with Applications, 39*, 11293–11302.

Chen, W., Guo, F., & Wang, F. Y. (2015). A survey of traffic data visualization. *IEEE Transactions on Intelligent Transportation Systems, 16*, 2970–2984.

Colombo, M., Hurle, S., Portmann, E., & Schäfer, E. (2020a). A framework for a crowdsourced creation of smart city wheels. In *2020 Seventh International Conference on eDemocracy and eGovernment (ICEDEG)* (pp. 305–308). IEEE.

Colombo, M., Nguyen, M. T., & Pincay, J. (2020b). Tutorial: Towards human-centered smart city solutions. In *2020 Seventh International Conference on eDemocracy and eGovernment (ICEDEG)* (pp. 3–5). IEEE.

D'Andrea, E., & Marcelloni, F. (2017). Detection of traffic congestion and incidents from GPS trace analysis. *Expert Systems with Applications, 73*, 43–56.

Gao, Y., & Wen, H.m. (2007). Technique and standardization research of radio data system-traffic message channel (RDS-TMC). *Journal of Transportation Systems Engineering and Information Technology, 3*, 49–54.

Haghrah, A. A., & Ghaemi, S. (2019). Pyit2fls: A new python toolkit for interval type 2 fuzzy logic systems.

Hudec, M. (2016). Fuzziness in information systems. In *Springer International Publishing* (pp. 67–99).

Hudec, M. (2019). Possibilities for linguistic summaries in cognitive cities. In *Designing Cognitive Cities* (pp. 47–84). Springer.

Karnik, N. N., & Mendel, J. M. (2001). Centroid of a type-2 fuzzy set. *Information Sciences, 132*, 195–220.

La Valley, R., Usher, A., & Cook, A. (2017). Detection of behavior patterns of interest using big data which have spatial and temporal attributes. *ISPRS Annals of Photogrammetry, Remote Sensing and Spatial Information Sciences, 4*, 31–35.

Li, L., Lin, W. H., & Liu, H. (2006). Type-2 fuzzy logic approach for short-term traffic forecasting. In *IEE Proceedings-Intelligent Transport Systems* (Vol. 153, pp. 33–40). IET.

Li, R., Jiang, C., Zhu, F., & Chen, X. (2016). Traffic flow data forecasting based on interval type-2 fuzzy sets theory. *IEEE/CAA Journal of Automatica Sinica, 3*, 141–148.

Liu, B. (2011). Uncertain logic for modeling human language. *Journal of Uncertain Systems, 5*, 3–20.

Lu, H., & Ooi, B.C. (1993). Spatial indexing: Past and future. *IEEE Data Engineering Bulletin, 16*, 16–21.

Maybury, M. (1999). *Advances in automatic text summarization.* MIT Press.

Mendel, J. M. (2007). Type-2 fuzzy sets and systems: An overview. *IEEE Computational Intelligence Magazine, 2*, 20–29.

Mináriková, E. (2021). Criteria for fuzzy rule-based systems and its applicability on examples. In *Proceedings of the 24th International Scientific Conference for Doctoral Students and Post-Doctoral Scholars (EDAMBA).* University of Economics in Bratislava.

Nagarajan, D., Lathamaheswari, M., Broumi, S., & Kavikumar, J. (2019). A new perspective on traffic control management using triangular interval type-2 fuzzy sets and interval neutrosophic sets. *Operations Research Perspectives, 6*, 100099.

Pang, L. X., Chawla, S., Liu, W., & Zheng, Y. (2013). On detection of emerging anomalous traffic patterns using gps data. *Data and Knowledge Engineering, 87*, 357–373.

Pedrycz, W. (2020). *An Introduction to Computing with Fuzzy Sets: Analysis, Design, and Applications* (Vol. 190). Springer.

Pedrycz, W., & Wang, X. (2015). Designing fuzzy sets with the use of the parametric principle of justifiable granularity. *IEEE Transactions on Fuzzy Systems, 24*, 489–496.

Pincay, J., Mensah, A., Portmann, E., & Terán, L. (2020). Forecasting travel times with space partitioning methods. In *Proceedings of the 6th International Conference on Geographical Information Systems Theory, Applications and Management—GISTAM* (pp. 151–159), INSTICC, SciTePress.

Pincay, J., Mensah, A. O., Portmann, E., & Terán, L. (2020a). Partitioning space to identify en-route movement patterns. In *2020 Seventh International Conference on eDemocracy and eGovernment (ICEDEG)* (pp. 43–49). IEEE.

Pincay, J., Portmann, E., & Terán, L. (2020b). Towards a computational intelligence framework to smartify the last-mile delivery. *POLIBITS, 62*, 85–91.

Pincay, J., Portmann, E., & Terán, L. (2021a). Fuzzifying geospatial data to identify critical traffic areas. In *Joint Proceedings of the 19th World Congress of the International Fuzzy Systems Association (IFSA), the 12th Conference of the European Society for Fuzzy Logic and Technology (EUSFLAT), and the 11th International Summer School on Aggregation Operators (AGOP)* (pp. 463–470). Atlantis Press.

Pincay, J., Portmann, E., & Terán, L. (2021b). Mining linguistic summaries in traffic. In *Proceedings of the 13th International Joint Conference on Computational Intelligence - FCTA* (pp. 169–176). INSTICC, SciTePress.

Popek, G., Kowalczyk, R., & Katarzyniak, R. P. (2011). Generating descriptions of incomplete city-traffic states with agents. In *Foundations of Intelligent Systems* (pp. 105–114). Springer.

Spolaor, S., Fuchs, C., Cazzaniga, P., Kaymak, U., Besozzi, D., & Nobile, M. S. (2020). Simpful: A user-friendly python library for fuzzy logic. *International Journal of Computational Intelligence Systems, 13*, 1687–1698.

Teodorović, D. (1994). Fuzzy sets theory applications in traffic and transportation. *European Journal of Operational Research, 74*, 379–390.

Thiagarajan, A., Ravindranath, L., Balakrishnan, H., Madden, S., & Girod, L. (2011). Accurate, low-energy trajectory mapping for mobile devices. In *Proceedings of the 8th USENIX conference on Networked systems design and implementation*. USENIX Association.

Trivino, G., Sanchez, A., Montemayor, A. S., Pantrigo, J. J., Cabido, R. & Pardo, E. G. (2010). Linguistic description of traffic in a roundabout. In *International Conference on Fuzzy Systems* (pp. 1–8). IEEE.

Vukovic, T. (2016). *Hilbert-Geohash-Hashing geographical point data using the Hilbert space-filling curve*. Master's thesis, NTNU.

Yuan, J., Zheng, Y., Xie, X., & Sun, G. (2011). Driving with knowledge from the physical world. In *Proceedings of the 17th ACM SIGKDD international conference on Knowledge discovery and data mining* (pp. 316–324). ACM.

Zadeh, L. A. (1975). The concept of a linguistic variable and its application to approximate reasoning II. *Information Sciences, 8*, 301–357.

Zadeh, L. A., Klir, G. J., & Yuan, B. (1996). *Fuzzy sets, fuzzy logic, and fuzzy systems: selected papers* (Vol. 6). World Scientific.

Chapter 5
Ethical Classification of Postal Customers

5.1 Conceptual Development

All Business to Consumer (B2C) companies that sell physical products via online stores face one common issue: planning the product delivery process. The last-mile delivery is a crucial step to complete the delivery operation successfully. Many challenges arise in this stage, with the main one being the successful delivery of a parcel to the customer on the first try. Every next try of delivery is an extra cost for the business since for home deliveries, this step usually depends on the customers being home.

In recent years, many solutions have been introduced to improve the success rate of first-try delivery. Such solutions include offering trunk delivery, parcel lockers, pickup places, and ad hoc carriers to the customers (Van Duin et al., 2016). Despite all of these alternatives, the majority of customers still prefer home delivery (Mangiaracina et al., 2019). In this regard, the main difficulty that the potential solutions face is the fact that it is hard to accurately predict where and when a customer is going to be at a particular time (Mangiaracina et al., 2019; Pan et al., 2017). Moreover, privacy is a significant concern; there are laws that need to be accomplished (e.g., GDPR[1]); moreover, most customers are not willing to share their location with companies.

There is thus a need to develop solutions that enable digital transformation and that follow an ethical behavior, even in traditional sectors such as the delivery industry. Therefore, efforts should be directed toward addressing the preceding issues and to implement digital-ethical solutions.

---

[1] https://gdpr-info.eu/.

5.2   Modeling Customer's Characteristics

The authors Mangiaracina et al. (2019) completed a literature review on increasing the last-mile delivery efficiency in B2C e-commerce. They reviewed 75 papers published between 2001 and 2019. Different approaches are mentioned in this review. One of them is *mapping customer behavior*. This solution is based on a data mining process to study the customer presence at home. This concept was referred to as very promising.

Another initiative is the one Pan et al. (2017), they have already studied ways of predicting whether the customer is at home or not, intending to improve the successful delivery rate of grocery orders placed online. They analyzed the electricity consumption patterns of the customers to make more efficient delivery plans. These plans were aimed at having higher probabilities of the customer being home while reducing travel costs. With this approach, the total travel distance could be reduced between 3% and 20% and the success rate of first-try deliveries was increased by around 18% and 26%. A big concern with such an approach is that it may arise legal issues since the privacy of the customers' data is at risk of violation.

In terms of profiling customers, the authors like Aryuni et al. (2018) and Lefait and Kechadi (2010) did some research on customer segmentation with clustering techniques. In both initiatives, customers were grouped into clusters based on the needs they had in common. More precisely, in Lefait and Kechadi (2010), the clustering was performed with actual data of the purchase behavior of customers. The dataset included 1000 customers and purchase behavior over 60 weeks for six different products. One challenge the researchers faced was choosing the proper clustering method, selecting at the end K-means because it was simpler to implement and quite efficient.

In Aryuni et al. (2018), the authors performed the customer segmentation on Internet banking. A Recency, Frequency, Monetary Value (RFM) score of customers' Internet banking transactions and two clustering methods, namely K-means and K-medoids, were used. After measuring and comparing the performance of these two approaches, they concluded that with K-means better results are obtained than with K-medoids.

In regard to classifying customers with fuzzy methods, in the work conducted by Kaufmann and Meier (2009), it was illustrated how a fuzzy-based approach was suitable to perform such a task. An Inductive Fuzzy Classification (IFC) method was compared to a crisp classification and random selection. Customers were divided into groups and were shown personalized advertisements of products that should best fit their needs. From the results, the customers classified with IFC were more likely to click on the ad (63% sales rate) compared to those classified by a crisp approach (30% sales rate) and random selection (20% sales rate). This difference in the performance between the crisp and fuzzy method was because the crisp method was not considering some characteristics that were used to perform the IFC classification. These results proved that fuzzy methods enable more close-to-reality and fair manners of performing customer analysis under certain circumstances.

In contrast to the existing approaches, this endeavor seeks to overcome privacy limitations by classifying customers based on their previous delivery history, provided that delivery companies already own the history of customers' past deliveries. To conclude which method allows that, three methods are compared: K-means clustering, fuzzy clustering, and a fuzzy-based classification model.

5.3 Methodology

Five main stages composed the method followed in the development of this research work: (i) data analysis, (ii) K-means clustering, (iii) fuzzy clustering, (iv) fuzzy inference, and (v) analysis of results. Figure 5.1 shows an overview of the methodology, its stages, and the main steps performed in each of them. After the data are cleaned, it is analyzed through 3 methods (stages ii, iii, and iv). After the results from each classification method are obtained, they are compared and evaluated, and the most appropriate classification of customers is selected. The details about them and the dataset used in developing the use case are presented in the following sections.

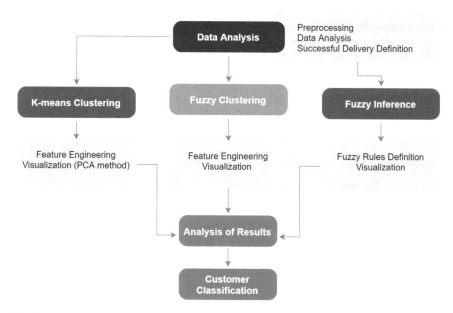

Fig. 5.1 Method followed in this study

5.3.1   Data Analysis

The dataset used in the development of the project was provided by the *Swiss Post*. It contained information about different events of deliveries in the city of Bern that took place during the years 2018, 2019, and half of 2020. For this study, the postal codes 3011 and 3013 were taken into consideration.

In total, there were 7,016,584 events in the initial dataset. Fourteen attributes described every event. After a careful examination, attributes containing information regarding the type of customer (i.e., natural or legal), street, house number, type of the event (e.g., delivered or not delivered), the way the delivery took place (e.g., given to the customer, left by the mailbox or by the door), and the date were taken into account. Records with missing or duplicated information were neglected, and only the ones that were targeted to natural persons (and not legal or companies) were kept; this consideration was taken since from the data, it was confirmed that deliveries to companies are more successful as they almost always have people around.

Furthermore, it was also necessary to define what a successful and what an unsuccessful delivery is, considering the information from the dataset:

- A *successful delivery* is a delivery that was handed directly to the customer at home.
- An *unsuccessful delivery* is a delivery that was not handed directly to the customer at home or is not delivered at all.

After this process, the dataset consisted of 453,076 deliveries to natural persons. Furthermore, for implementation purposes, only spring months (March, April, and May) were considered, resulting in 1786 customers and 30,675 deliveries.

In the following sections, specifics about the implementation of the different methods used for analysis are presented.

5.3.2   K-means Clustering

Customers were classified based on their past deliveries to notice patterns of when a delivery is more likely to be successful. A crisp classification method, namely the K-means method, was applied. Moreover, the Elbow method (Syakur et al., 2018) was used to determine an appropriate number of clusters; then, a dimensionality reduction method was applied to visualize the discovered clusters. The details are provided next.

5.3.2.1   Feature Engineering

From the deliveries obtained as a result of the data analysis stage, only the *successful deliveries* were considered since the profile is built upon past successful events. It was then determined that the most critical field in the dataset for the classification is the date and time of when the successful delivery was made. Thus, it was decided to use a discretized version of the date to represent it better.

Weekdays and times from each successful delivery date were extracted. The times were then mapped into the dayparts: morning (07:00–10:00), noon (11:00–12:00), afternoon (14:00–16:00), and evening (17:00–20:00). Afterward, every household or customer is described in terms of 23 features, since the delivery services are offered only six days a week (Monday to Saturday), and no deliveries take place on Saturday evening.

5.3.2.2   K-means Clustering

Following some recommendations on the literature (Aryuni et al., 2018; Lefait & Kechadi, 2010), the K-means clustering method was selected. Besides, the random method, which chooses the initial centroids of clusters randomly, was implemented. To select a suitable number of clusters, experiments with different values of k were performed. After observing the results, $k = 4$ was chosen as the number of clusters suitable to the data available. It was also later confirmed with the Elbow method that this was the correct number.

Furthermore, the features of each centroid were ranked to obtain their main characteristics.

5.3.2.3   Visualization

Visualizing 23 dimensions for the 23 features used in the K-means is not possible. Thus, a dimensionality reduction method was needed to transform our data from a 23-dimensional space to a 2-dimensional (representable) space. The Principal Component Analysis (PCA) method Wold et al. (1987) was applied since it is straightforward to implement and enables the extraction of the most representative features.

5.3.3   Fuzzy Clustering

K-means is a crisp classification method, meaning that one element can belong to only one group. Fuzzy clustering, on the other hand, takes concepts from fuzzy sets meaning that one element can belong to more than one cluster to a certain degree. This property enables to represent in a better way an uncertain concept such as the presence of a customer at home at a particular part of the day. For instance, a person could be *sometimes* at home in the morning or *often*; such characteristics could be difficult to capture with a hard clustering method since the classification in such a case will be either at home or not.

Further details about the classification with fuzzy clustering are presented below.

5.3.3.1   Feature Engineering and Cluster Validation

For the selection of features, a similar selection and definition process as the one presented in Sect. 5.3.2.2 was conducted.

One crucial aspect that has to be considered for fuzzy clustering is defining the number of clusters and measuring their validity. To that end, three validity metrics were applied: fuzzy partition coefficient, generalized silhouette, and fuzzy partition entropy.

The fuzzy partition coefficient is defined in the range from 0 to 1. When the fuzzy partition value is maximized, the data are represented more adequately by the correspondent value of the number of clusters. The fuzzy partition coefficient is formally defined by Eq. 5.1 (Trauwaert, 1988).

$$fpc = \frac{\sum_{c=1}^{C} \sum_{i=1}^{N} u_{ci}^2}{N} \tag{5.1}$$

where C is the number of clusters, and N is the number of data points.

On the other hand, the generalized silhouette helps approximate the optimal number of clusters by considering a fuzzy partition matrix to identify areas with higher data densities. The generalized silhouette is formally defined by Eq. 5.2 (Rawashdeh & Ralescu, 2012).

$$s_j = \frac{a_j - b_j}{\max(a_j, b_j)} \tag{5.2}$$

where s_j is the silhouette value, a_j is the compactness distance, and b_j is the separation distance. The distances a_j and b_j are defined as follows:

$$a_j = min \left\{ \frac{\sum_{k=1}^{n} IntraDist_i(j,k) \cdot d_{jk}}{\sum_{k=1}^{n} IntraDist_i(j,k)} \mid i = 1, \ldots, c \right\} \tag{5.3}$$

$$b_j = min \left\{ \frac{\sum_{k=1}^{n} InterDist_{rs}(j,k) \cdot d_{jk}}{\sum_{k=1}^{n} InterDist_{rs}(j,k)} \mid r, s = 1, \ldots, c \text{ and } r < s \right\} \tag{5.4}$$

s_j takes the values in $[-1, 1]$. If the value of s_j is positive, meaning that b_j is larger than a_j, then the clustering approach is good. Otherwise, it means that it needs to be adjusted.

The fuzzy partition entropy is a scalar measure of the amount of fuzziness in a given dataset. The optimal number of clusters C is found solving Eq. 5.5 (Bezdek, 1974).

$$fpe = \frac{\sum_{c=1}^{C} \sum_{i=1}^{N} u_{ci} \log(u_{ci})}{-N} \qquad (5.5)$$

where C is the number of clusters, and N is the number of data points.

With the results of these three metrics and varying the features, it was possible to perform the clustering process and the classification.

5.3.3.2 Visualization

Similarly, for the K-means clustering procedure, visualizing all the dimensions for all the features is not possible. The PCA method was also applied in this case to represent and visualize the most representative features.

5.3.4 Fuzzy Inference

Similar to the artifacts designed in Chap. 4, it was opted to implement a fuzzy inference system but applied it to the presence of the customers at home. The primary motivation behind this was that fuzzy reasoning and inference represent in a better way how humans make decisions (see Chap. 3) than non-supervised methods such as clustering. Thus, it was sought to confirm if the results obtained by this method were more appropriate than the likes of the clustering approaches.

To achieve such a goal, it was necessary to define rules for the inference process and find an appropriate way of visualizing the results. The details about these steps are presented in the following sections.

5.3.4.1 Fuzzy Rules Definition

Given the large number of features, it was opted to analyze the success of deliveries in the morning. To that effect, 5 features were defined as the antecedents of the fuzzy rules: *Monday morning*, *Tuesday morning*, *Wednesday morning*, *Thursday morning*, and *Friday morning*. The output depicted the success of delivery in the morning hours.

The input variables corresponded to the success of past deliveries on all the days of the week, for instance, *delivery never successful in Monday morning*, *delivery mostly successful in Wednesday morning*, and *delivery always successful on Friday morning*. The output corresponds to the overall success of the delivery in the morning, for example, *delivery always successful in the morning* or *delivery mostly successful in the morning*, outcomes that are computed according to the features of every customer.

Furthermore, the consequents of the fuzzy rules were defined following this reasoning:

- If the deliveries are always successful in all five mornings, then the customer is always in the mornings at home.
- If the deliveries are always successful at least two mornings in a week and are primarily successful the other days, then the customer is mostly in the mornings at home.
- If the deliveries are always successful at least two or three mornings in a week and are rarely or sometimes successful the other days, then the customer is sometimes in the mornings at home.
- If the deliveries are mostly successful at least three mornings in a week and are rarely successful the other days, then the customer is sometimes in the mornings at home.
- If the deliveries are never successful at least two mornings in a week and are rarely successful the other days, then the customer is never in the mornings at home.
- If the deliveries are never successful, then the customer is never in the mornings at home.

The results of the inference were computed with the Mamdani inference model and defuzzified with the centroid method (see Sect. 3.1.4).

5.3.4.2 Visualization

Visualizing the membership degrees of the customers to the different sets of the output is not a trivial task. For the K-means and the fuzzy clustering, a PCA-based method was used. Nevertheless, the method does not represent the membership degrees correctly. For that reason, it was chosen to perform the visualization of results with a membership network. This method was used successfully to represent high-dimensional data as it was shown in Ariza-Jiménez et al. (2019).

The results of the implementation of the previously described methods are presented in the following section.

5.4   Implementation and Results

This section presents the results of implementing the classification methods following the methods explained in the previous section.

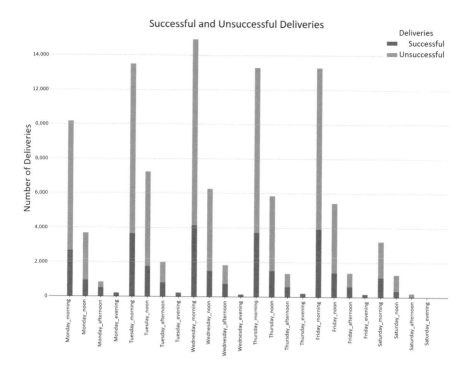

Fig. 5.2 Distribution of successful and unsuccessful deliveries obtained from the studied dataset. Adapted from Jaha et al. (2021)

The data analysis and the methods to perform the classification were implemented in the programming language Python. It was confirmed that the percentage of unsuccessful deliveries is higher than the successful ones for natural customers. Moreover, after segmenting the data by time window, it was observed that most deliveries take place in the morning and at noon and that the proportion of unsuccessful events is also larger than when the attempts take place in the afternoon and the evening. Figure 5.2 presents how the delivery events elapsed during the studied period, having only 26.16% parcels delivered successfully on the first try.

These results backed the decision of analyzing the data by dayparts to perform the selection of features.

The outcome of the classification obtained with K-means, fuzzy clustering, and fuzzy inference is presented next.

Table 5.1 K-means cluster characteristics. Adapted from Jaha et al. (2021)

Rank	Cluster A	Cluster B	Cluster C	Cluster D
1.	Wednesday_morning	Friday_morning	Tuesday_morning	Wednesday_morning
2.	Friday_morning	Wednesday_morning	Wednesday_morning	Friday_morning
3.	Thursday_morning	Thursday_morning	Thursday_morning	Tuesday_morning
4.	Tuesday_morning	Tuesday_morning	Monday_morning	Thursday_morning
5.	Monday_morning	Monday_morning	Friday_morning	Monday_morning

Table 5.2 Top feature per daypart of each cluster. Adapted from Jaha et al. (2021)

Dayparts	Cluster A	Cluster B	Cluster C	Cluster D
Morning	Wednesday_morning	Friday_morning	Tuesday_morning	Wednesday_morning
Noon	Tuesday_noon	Thursday_noon	Friday_noon	Tuesday_noon
Afternoon	Tuesday_afternoon	Tuesday_afternoon	Friday_afternoon	Tuesday_afternoon
Evening	Tuesday_evening	Monday_evening	Friday_evening	Thursday_evening

5.4.1 Customer Classification with K-means Clustering

The implementation of the K-means clustering was made on `Python` with the library `Pandas`[2] and the machine learning library `Sklearn`.[3]

After the clustering process was applied and as per the results of the Elbow method (see Sect. 5.3.2.2), 4 clusters were obtained through the K-means method. Table 5.1 depicts the top 5 features of each centroid of the resulting clusters. Worth noticing is that the characteristics of the centroids do not have much variety regarding the dayparts (i.e., all of them are in the morning). It was assumed that this result is because most packages are attempted to be delivered during that part of the day.

To have more variety of characteristics of the clusters and for analysis purposes, the highest ranked feature per each daypart was determined. Table 5.2 presents the obtained results.

As to the distribution of the number of customers in each cluster, Cluster A grouped 438, Cluster B 1313, Cluster C 1, and Cluster D 34 customers. Figure 5.3 allows visualizing the clusters, whose dimensions have been reduced using the PCA method provided by `sklearn`. Worth noticing is that the Cluster C can be considered a cluster of isolated values as it contains only one element.

---

[2] https://pandas.pydata.org/.

[3] https://scikit-learn.org/stable/.

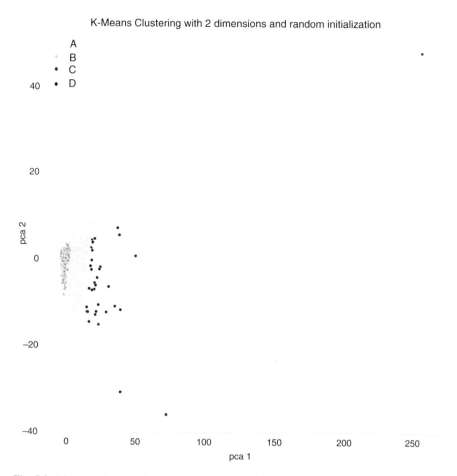

Fig. 5.3 PCA visualization of the customers in each of the clusters described in Table 5.1. Taken from Jaha et al. (2021)

5.4.2 Customer Classification with Fuzzy Clustering

The fuzzy clustering algorithm was implemented using the Skfuzzy[4] library for Python.

As presented in Sect. 5.3.2.2, three metrics were evaluated to define the number of clusters and their validity. In Fig. 5.4 (top), it can be observed that the highest value the fuzzy partition coefficient has is when the number of clusters is 2; in Fig. 5.4 (center) when the number of clusters is 2, the generalized silhouette achieves its highest value; and at last, in Fig. 5.4 (bottom), the fuzzy partition entropy has the

---

[4] https://pythonhosted.org/scikit-fuzzy/.

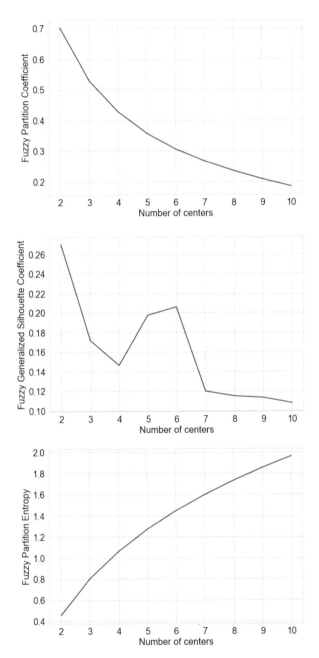

Fig. 5.4 Evaluation of fuzzy partition coefficient (top), generalized silhouette (center), and fuzzy partition entropy (bottom) to identify and validate the number of clusters

Table 5.3 Fuzzy clusters
characteristics

Rank	Cluster FA	Cluster FB
1.	Tuesday_afternoon	Saturday_morning
2.	Friday_afternoon	Tuesday_evening
3.	Wednesday_afternoon	Thursday_evening
4.	Monday_afternoon	Tuesday_afternoon
5.	Saturday_morning	Thursday_afternoon

Table 5.4 Fuzzy cluster
characteristics split into
dayparts

Daypart	Fuzzy Cluster A	Fuzzy Cluster B
Morning	Saturday_morning	Saturday_morning
Noon	Thursday_noon	Saturday_noon
Afternoon	Tuesday_afternoon	Tuesday_afternoon
Evening	Thursday_evening	Tuesday_evening

smallest value when the number of clusters is 2. Based on these results, the optimal
number of clusters with the mentioned features was 2.

Table 5.3 shows the characteristics of the two clusters obtained with fuzzy
clustering. Each of the clusters exhibits the top 5 features.

When comparing the two clusters, it can be observed that there is no variety in
the dayparts. In Cluster FA, the daypart afternoon appears four out of five times.
On the other hand, in Cluster FB, the daypart afternoon came just as often as the
daypart evening. In a similar manner as in the case of the K-means clustering, the
top feature for each daypart was computed. The results are presented in Table 5.4.
As it can be observed, for the daypart morning and afternoon, the outcome is the
same in both clusters.

The PCA method was used again to visualize the clusters. Unfortunately, this
method allows to represent the fuzzy clusters discretely, and thus the membership
degrees of the elements to the clusters cannot be appreciated (Fig. 5.5).

5.4.3   Customer Classification with Fuzzy Inference

As previously explained (see Sect. 5.3.4), for the fuzzy inference, only five features
were chosen. They corresponded to the success of deliveries in the morning.
Unfortunately, having a large number of features (23) leads to a large number
of rules (curse of dimensionality (Hudec, 2016)), and thus the inference problem
becomes cumbersome. However, the same procedure used for the mornings could
be applied to the other parts of the day when needed.

The fuzzy inference for customer classification was implemented as well in
Python and the library Simpful was used to program the antecedents, consequents, and rules of the system.

The values of the antecedents on the database were computed considering the
total number of orders in a period versus the total number of successful deliveries.

Fig. 5.5 PCA visualization of the fuzzy clusters

The antecedents were defined using the fuzzy sets presented in Fig. 5.6 and the output with the fuzzy sets depicted in Fig. 5.7.

Given the number of features and possible combinations, 868 rules were defined. A sample of the code for the definition of the fuzzy rules can be found in Appendix C.

Furthermore, as it was a goal to represent the groups of customers visually, a membership network was created based on the inference process for each studied customer. Figure 5.8 depicts the Membership Network created with the Gephi Software.[5] Each output set is represented in the graph with a different color; the small circles (nodes) represent the customers, and the closer they are to the center, the higher the membership degree. The nodes that have links with more of one set imply that they belong in some degree to both. Lastly, a database with the

---

[5] https://gephi.org/.

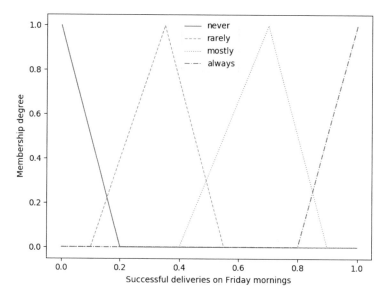

Fig. 5.6 Fuzzy sets for the input variables of the inference for customer classification

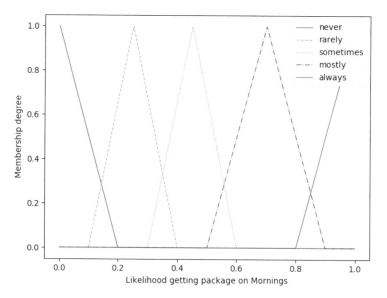

Fig. 5.7 Fuzzy sets for the output of the inference for customer classification

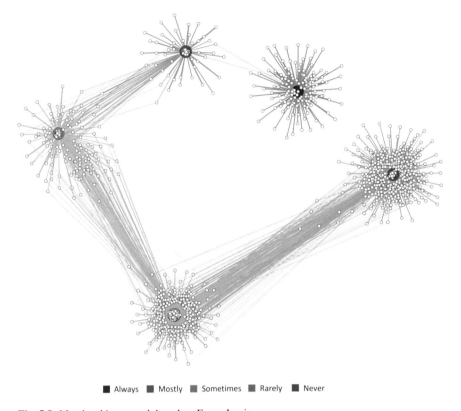

■ Always ■ Mostly ■ Sometimes ■ Rarely ■ Never

Fig. 5.8 Membership network based on Fuzzy Logic

membership degrees of each customer to the fuzzy sets was obtained. This outcome constituted the classification of the customers.

5.4.3.1   Verification of the Design Criteria for Fuzzy Sets

As it was presented in Sect. 3.1.5.2, some specific criteria and constraints need to be followed to guarantee that the defined fuzzy sets depict reality adequately.

The criteria of normality, continuity, and convexity were verified for the fuzzy sets that were previously defined for the input and output of the fuzzy inference system for the customer classification. All of them were met. The criteria for designing linguistic variables were also met.

Since a fuzzy inference system was used to classify the customers, the design constraints for fuzzy rules were also verified:

1. *Rule length:* This rule states that the number of fuzzy should be as small as possible. This criterion was hard to meet given that the four variables constitute the antecedents of the rules, and each of them has 4 linguistic labels. It was tried

to reduce the number of rules by applying the reasoning explained in Sect. 5.3.4; however, still the resulting number of rules was high, and therefore this criterion is partially met.

2. *Local models:* The rules were designed in a way that the consequents represent a direct effect of all of the antecedents in a way that they can be understood. Hence, this criterion follows the local models constraint definition.

3. *Granular consequents:* The outputs of all the rules are represented by linguistic terms. Thus, this criterion is accomplished.

5.5 Analysis of Results

This section conducts a review and analysis of the results obtained by the three classification methods.

From the classification with hard clustering, 4 clusters were obtained. The number of clusters was defined with the Elbow method (Syakur et al., 2018). The features obtained per each cluster showed that the customers belonging to them are more frequently reached during the mornings. However, this result can be considered as predictable, given that from the dataset, most of the deliveries take place during the morning and noon. Furthermore, as per the validation of the results through a recommendation engine performed in Jaha et al. (2021), an accuracy of only 21% for this classification was obtained. This result hints that this classification method, although straightforward to implement, might not be adequate.

When performing a fuzzy variation of clustering, the outcome was unexpected. Even though the dataset was the same as in the previous case, only two clusters were obtained after validating and defining the number of clusters with three metrics. Their characteristics were different from the ones obtained from the K-means approach. It was considered that having only two groups might not be suitable to perform a classification since even one is using fuzzy methods, the outcome is similar to a dichotomy. Causes for this result can be the nature of the data, and possibly a more extensive feature engineering had to be performed.

On the other hand, the classification obtained by means of the fuzzy inference system required more preparation work than the clustering approaches. Furthermore, given the number of features, it was necessary only to analyze one daypart. This consideration constitutes the main weakness of this method. However, the classification process was performed more naturally and represented better the randomness of a concept, such as the presence of a person at home. The system was validated, verifying the design constraints and guidelines for fuzzy sets and fuzzy rules and against a test set. To perform so, the year 2020 was removed from the dataset used to perform the classification; then the results were compared to what was indeed happened in 2020. The new results showed an accuracy of around 80%, which can be considered successful for this type of analysis. Thus, this classification method and results were selected to achieve the goals of this research project.

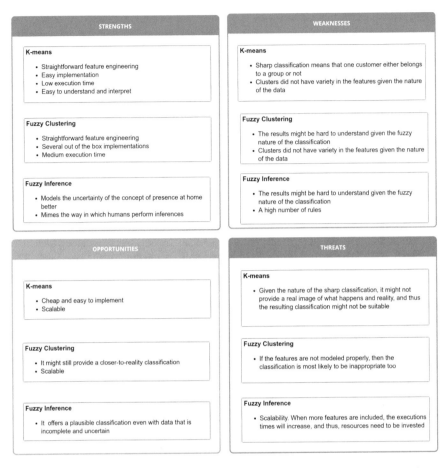

Fig. 5.9 SWOT analysis of the classification of customers performed with K-means, fuzzy clustering, and fuzzy inference

Furthermore, Fig. 5.9 summarizes the findings after the analysis process of the three methods in the form of a SWOT analysis (analysis of strengths, weakness, opportunities, and threats).

As per the results of the SWOT analysis and inspection of the outcome of the three methods, it was decided that the most appropriate approach to classifying the customers with the available was with the fuzzy inference model.

5.6   Conclusions and Lessons Learned

With the implementation of this artifact, it was sought to classify postal customers with data that do not compromise their privacy (i.e., that is not derived from a constant tracking of geographical location). The motivation for this was to demonstrate how such a task is achievable even when the data available are not precise but still allow obtaining good results and, with that, contribute with a digital-ethical solution.

With the outcome of the three conducted analyses, it is possible to claim that crisp classification methods (such as the K-means clustering), although simple to implement and understand, may not be adequate to perform a task with the type of data used in this project. Moreover, special attention should be given to feature engineering since it directly influences the quality of the results. As it was presented, even the fuzzy variation of the clustering algorithm did not provide satisfactory results.

Using fuzzy reasoning and inference as a way of imitating the way humans think proved to offer better results and thus confirming the notion of the author about the suitability of fuzzy and CI methods to derive knowledge from incomplete and uncertain information. However, feature engineering also plays an essential role in this case since it may lead to an explosion of the number of rules of the system.

For the particularities of this case study, the following was concluded in light of the results obtained:

- The delivery company follows a relatively fixed schedule of delivery (i.e., mostly before noon), and thus, from the dataset, it could be derived that the most successful part of the day to deliver is during the morning, although only 30% of the attempts are successful for natural persons.
- This already established delivery schedule makes it hard to extract meaningful information from the dataset when using clustering. Given that most of the deliveries are successful in the morning, and thus the clusters might not have that many different features.
- Human behavior changes over time, making it challenging to predict when a customer might be at home. Therefore, we consider that more approximate methods should be employed in the development of solutions.

Furthermore, it was not possible to perform a more exhaustive evaluation for all the approaches (i.e., with a real-life simulation), given that this project was developed when restrictions of mobility due to the COVID-19 pandemic were in place.

However, thanks to the exchange with the data partners and the data validations performed, the author claims that they are still valuable, and the insights obtained can still be leveraged to achieve the goals of improving the last-mile delivery.

With the results presented in this chapter and Chap. 4, it was possible to define a framework to achieve this goal. Further details are presented in the next part of this book.

5.7 Further Readings

- **Rokach and Maimon (2005).** "This chapter presents a tutorial overview of the main clustering methods used in Data Mining. The goal is to provide a self-contained review of the concepts and the mathematics underlying clustering techniques" (abs.).
- **Miyamoto et al. (2008).** "The main subject of this book is the fuzzy c-means proposed by Dunn and Bezdek and their variations including recent studies. A main reason why we concentrate on fuzzy c-means is that most methodology and application studies in fuzzy clustering use fuzzy c-means, and hence fuzzy c-means should be considered to be a major technique of clustering in general, regardless whether one is interested in fuzzy methods or not" (abs.).

References

Ariza-Jiménez, L., Villa, L.F. & Quintero, O.L. (2019). Memberships networks for high-dimensional fuzzy clustering visualization. In *Workshop on Engineering Applications* (pp. 263–273). Springer.

Aryuni, M., Madyatmadja, E.D. & Miranda, E. (2018). Customer segmentation in xyz bank using k-means and k-medoids clustering. In *2018 International Conference on Information Management and Technology (ICIMTech)* (pp. 412–416). IEEE.

Bezdek, J. (1974). Cluster validity with fuzzy sets j. *Cybernet.*

Hudec, M. (2016). *Fuzziness in information systems* (pp. 67–99). Springer International Publishing .

Jaha, A., Jaha, D., Pincay, J., Terán, L. & Portmann, E. (2021). Privacy-friendly delivery plan recommender. In *2021 Eighth International Conference on eDemocracy eGovernment (ICEDEG)* (pp. 146–151).

Kaufmann, M. & Meier, A. (2009). An inductive fuzzy classification approach applied to individual marketing. In *NAFIPS 2009-2009 Annual Meeting of the North American Fuzzy Information Processing Society* (pp. 1–6). IEEE.

Lefait, G. & Kechadi, T. (2010). Customer segmentation architecture based on clustering techniques. In *2010 Fourth International Conference on Digital Society* (pp. 243–248). IEEE.

Mangiaracina, R., Perego, A., Seghezzi, A. & Tumino, A. (2019). Innovative solutions to increase last-mile delivery efficiency in b2c e-commerce: a literature review. *International Journal of Physical Distribution & Logistics Management.*

Miyamoto, S., Ichihashi, H., Honda, K. & Ichihashi, H. (2008). *Algorithms for fuzzy clustering.* Springer.

Pan, S., Giannikas, V., Han, Y., Grover-Silva, E. & Qiao, B. (2017). Using customer-related data to enhance e-grocery home delivery. *Industrial Management & Data Systems.*

Rawashdeh, M. & Ralescu, A. (2012). Crisp and fuzzy cluster validity: Generalized intra-inter silhouette index. In *2012 Annual Meeting of the North American Fuzzy Information Processing Society (NAFIPS)* (pp. 1–6).

Rokach, L. & Maimon, O. (2005). Clustering methods. In *Data mining and knowledge discovery handbook* (pp. 321–352). Springer.

Syakur, M., Khotimah, B., Rochman, E. & Satoto, B. (2018). Integration k-means clustering method and elbow method for identification of the best customer profile cluster. In *IOP Conference Series: Materials Science and Engineering* (vol. 336, p. 012017). IOP Publishing.

Trauwaert, E. (1988). On the meaning of dunn's partition coefficient for fuzzy clusters. *Fuzzy Sets and Systems, 25,* 217–242.

Van Duin, J., De Goffau, W., Wiegmans, B., Tavasszy, L. & Saes, M. (2016). Improving home delivery efficiency by using principles of address intelligence for b2c deliveries. *Transportation Research Procedia, 12,* 14–25.

Wold, S., Esbensen, K. & Geladi, P. (1987). Principal component analysis. *Chemometrics and Intelligent Laboratory Systems, 2,* 37–52.

Part IV
Framework and Implementation

Chapter 6
The Fuzzy Ant Routing (FAR) Conceptual Framework

6.1 Background

While most delivery companies have optimized the majority of their distribution channels, there is still a lack of effective models for the optimization of the so-called *last-mile delivery*. According to several authors (e.g., Mańdziuk (2018); Mangiaracina et al. (2019) and Lim et al. (2018)), the last mile is the component of the supply chains, which has the most potential to be optimized and give an advantage to retailers and delivery companies. At the same time, it is the most challenging to address.

Despite all the existing solutions and alternatives given to customers (e.g., pick-up places, ad hoc carriers, trunk delivery, and parcel lockers), home delivery is the first choice of the vast majority of people. Therefore, efforts should still be directed toward addressing the issues above.

The Fuzzy Ant Routing (FAR) conceptual framework seeks to pride a schema that allows improving the first-try delivery by studying the behavior of traffic on the streets and customers' presence at home. In contrast to existing solutions, it is proposed to work only with data that do not compromise the customers' privacy (i.e., avoiding the use of location tracking data) and to get insights about traffic characteristics without the need of deploying a large number of vehicles or expensive sensors to obtain data. The main goal is to provide a delivery route plan to the delivery team and route planners, which allows delivering the highest quantity of parcels during the first try. Such capability will be translated into fewer resources consumption and possibly increased customer satisfaction.

The goal of designing a routing plan under uncertainty and with inaccurate data can be achieved by implementing fuzzy logic and computational intelligence methods. Furthermore, the FAR framework was developed following the principles of the design science research for information systems methodology (Hevner et al., 2004) and with a transdisciplinary approach (i.e., incorporating practical experiences into the solution process (Hadorn et al., 2008)).

6.2   Outline of the Framework

The notion behind the conceptualization of the FAR framework is the one of enabling the representation of data depicting concepts such as traffic level or how often a person is in a place through fuzzy methods. This process enables obtaining insights about characteristics and restrictions that should be considered when creating a delivery plan. Moreover, the results should be as well provided in an understandable and accessible manner to the end-users. Thus, the FAR framework was conceptualized with four key layers: *Data* Layer, *Knowledge* Layer, *Intelligence* Layer, and *Visualization* Layer. Figure 6.1 depicts the FAR framework's modular architecture. The details are provided next.

- The *Data Layer* contains the different data sources. Possible data sources that can be used for last-mile delivery are the history of successful deliveries to customers and the vehicles' log of events during service hours. This, however, can be adapted depending on the domain or specific circumstances.
- The *Knowledge Layer* takes data from the Data Layer and processes it through fuzzy logic methods. The output of this layer is a fuzzy classification of the input data and it can be used to make inferences or decisions. Examples of outputs are a traffic score for a specific zone at a particular time (e.g., zone with high traffic or zone with regular traffic) and the depiction of the success of delivery at a specific part of the day (e.g., delivery sometimes successful in the mornings).
- The output from the Knowledge Layer serves as input for the *Intelligence Layer* and it constitutes the basis to compute and find the most convenient routes. This layer can implement any swarm intelligence algorithm. In this particular case, the fuzzy ant system described in Sect. 3.2.3 is used to find the best candidate routes,

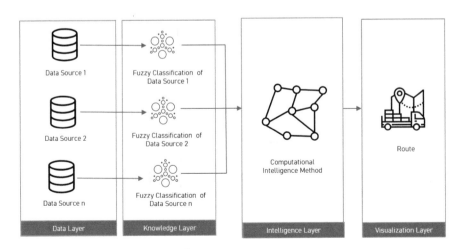

Fig. 6.1 FAR framework architecture[*]
[*]All icons included are from the thenounproject.com used under Creative Commons license

considering the classification and characteristics of the data obtained from the knowledge layer.

- The *Visualization Layer* allows displaying the top-performing delivery route(s) that enables delivering the highest amount of parcels in a specific time frame.

In the coming sections, further details of all the layers of the FAR conceptual framework and its components are described.

6.3 Architecture and Component Interaction

This section elaborates on the details of the different layers that integrate the FAR conceptual framework.

6.3.1 Data Layer

The Data Layer contains the different data sources necessary to perform the computations. Their nature depends on the problem domain. They can be stored in databases, data warehouses, or even some format for data transportation and exchange (e.g., CSV or XML).

For the specific case of the last-mile delivery, geospatial traffic-related data and history of deliveries are considered to illustrate this framework. To ease the reading, when referring to the geospatial traffic-related data, the acronym DS_1 is adopted, whereas the acronym DS_2 is used to refer to the delivery history database.

6.3.2 Knowledge Layer

The methods for extracting information from the data sources of the Data Layer depend on their nature. Taking, for instance, the DS_1, one can understand how traffic on the streets behaves at specific dayparts or identify traffic areas with more traffic than others. On the other hand, with the DS_2, it is possible to approximate the customer behavior.

DS_1 and DS_2 depict data that describe non-precise information. For the case of DS_1, concepts such as *heavy traffic* or *normal traffic* can be extracted; in a similar manner for DS_2, the success of past deliveries can be described as *always successful* or *sometimes successful*).

To deal with such concepts and make computations, computational intelligence methods can be applied (e.g., fuzzy sets and fuzzy clustering). Fuzzy sets, fuzzy inferences, and the definition of linguistic variables are the methods that are

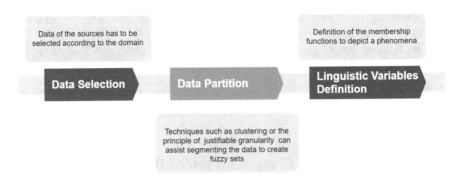

Fig. 6.2 Knowledge Layer process

exploited in the design of the FAR framework given their versatility when addressing imprecision and ambiguity, as explained in Chapter 3.

Figure 6.2 describes the process that the Knowledge Layer conducts. It consists of three stages:

1. *Data Selection*: Implies selecting relevant data representing phenomena or the problem that needs to be addressed.
2. *Data Partition*: Consists of segmenting the data to identify groups of similar characteristics that might define fuzzy sets. Methods such as clustering or the parametric principle of justifiable granularity can be applied (Pedrycz & Wang, 2015). It should be highlighted that with any method used, the fuzzy set has to come with well-formed semantics (Pedrycz, 2020).
3. *Linguistic Variables Definition*: They depict the observations about a phenomenon or situation in natural words and are defined upon the membership function describing the fuzzy sets obtained in the previous step.

As an example of the outcome of the Knowledge Layer, from the DS_1, the traffic conditions can be represented in terms of linguistic variables such as *low traffic*, *normal traffic*, *heavy traffic*, and *very heavy traffic*, while in the case of the data of the DS_2 the delivery success of parcels in the household could be defined as *always unsuccessful*, *sometimes successful*, *most of the times successful*, and *always successful*. Possible membership functions of such fuzzy sets are shown in Figs. 6.3 and 6.4.

6.3.3 Intelligence Layer

The Intelligence Layer is responsible for determining the best performing routes to cover the package delivery from the last mile.

The FAS proposes the usage of linguistic variables to approximate the distance between nodes when deciding which place to visit (see Sect. 3.2.3). Taking that

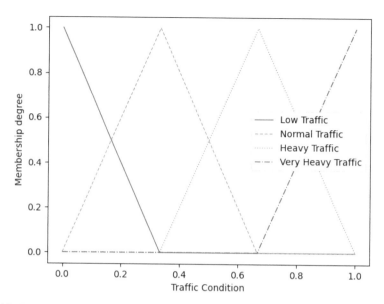

Fig. 6.3 Example of membership functions of the fuzzy sets depicting traffic conditions

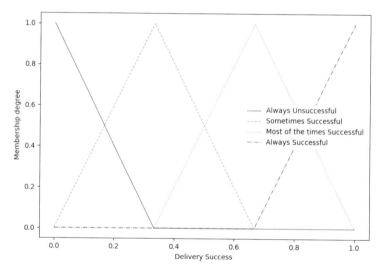

Fig. 6.4 Membership functions of the fuzzy sets depicting delivery success of parcels in a household

approach further and landing it to the last-mile delivery, the FAR framework attempts to propose a schema for practical implementation on the boundary of the principles of FAS, by adding other variables that come into play when performing the delivery of packages to households.

Such variables include the distance between locations to visit, the traffic conditions, the history of the delivery success, and the pheromone along with the links (see Sect. 3.2.2). For the traffic conditions and the history of delivery success, their linguistic definitions were presented in the previous section. In the case of the distance between locations and the pheromone levels, they can be represented in a similar manner. For the case of the distance, it can be depicted as *short, medium,* and *long*. For the pheromone intensity, the concepts of *weak, medium,* and *strong* are adopted. Figure 6.5 illustrates the membership functions for the distance and the pheromone intensity.

As an example, when an ant has to decide about the utility of the following link, meaning in this context the following address to visit to deliver a package, it can act per fuzzy rules composed in the following manner:

If d_{ij} is SMALL and τ_{ij} is STRONG and ϕ_j is ALWAYS SUCCESSFUL and
    θ_{ij} is NO TRAFFIC
Then u_{ij} is VERY HIGH

where d_{ij} is the distance between node i and node j, τ_{ij} represents the pheromone along with the link (i, j), ϕ_j represents the delivery success of the customer located in node j, θ_{ij} is the traffic status when transiting from node i to j, and finally, u_{ij} corresponds to the ant's perceived utility when choosing the node j considering that current location of the ant is the node i.

The usage of fuzzy rules of this type will address the issues that partially known input brings along.

Furthermore, adapting the FAS of Teodorović and Lučić (2005, 2007) algorithm to the conditions of the problem addressed in this work, the top-performing route is created following Algorithm 6.1:

6.3.4 Visualization Layer

The Visualization Layer enables displaying the top-performing route to deliver the highest amount of parcels. The visualization can be done through any interface; for the sake of the FAR framework, a web interface with a map was chosen.

The delivery team and the planners can observe the recommended route in a specific time window through the map.

6.4 Evaluation Design

As per the design science methodology guidelines, it is necessary to demonstrate a designed artifact's utility, quality, and efficacy through some method. The business environment in which the artifact will work defines the requirements of such evaluation, and thus, the evaluation entails the integration of new IT artifacts

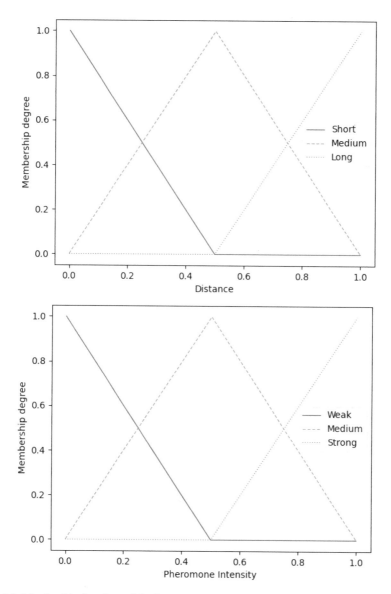

Fig. 6.5 Membership functions of the fuzzy sets depicting distance between locations (left) and pheromone intensity (right)

within the technical infrastructure of the business environment (Hevner et al., 2004; Kuechler & Vaishnavi, 2008).

Based on the above and given the nature of the delivery business, a *case study* evaluation, meaning to study the artifact in-depth business environment and observe how it behaves, would have been an appropriate way of assessing the utility, quality,

---

Algorithm 6.1 FAS algorithm for the FAR theoretical framework in pseudocode

---

Input: Linguistic variable T describing traffic conditions
Input: Linguistic variable D describing delivery success
Input: Linguistic variable DL describing distance between locations
Input: Linguistic variable P describing pheromone intensity
Input: List of locations to visit l
Output: Top-performing route r
  1: Set the counter of the cycles to zero ($c = 0$)
  2: Define the number the numbers of cycles c that the algorithm is going to be executed.
  3: Compute the distance between the locations l lo visit
  4: **repeat**
  5:     Set the counter of ants to one ($k = 1$)
  6:     Locate m ants at the starting point
  7:     Generate m routes to be visited by the m ants
  8:     When all nodes of a route are visited, ant k will finish with the route design
  9:     Increase the ant counter by one after creating the route
10:     Update pheromone trail
11:     **if** The ant counter is equal to $m + 1$ **then**
12:       Increase cycle counter c by one
13:       Update pheromone trail
14:     **end if**
15: **until** The number of cycles c is reached
16: **return** The top performing route that allow a higher delivery hit-ratio r with the shortest tour length

---

and efficacy of an instance of the FAR conceptual framework. However, given that the last stages of the development of this book took place during the first year and a half of the Covid-19 pandemic, it was not possible to conduct such an observational evaluation method.

It was opted then to design an evaluation method using an experimental approach, namely a *simulation*. It is possible to evaluate how an artifact behaves under certain conditions and with specific data through simulations. Even though it might not be the ideal way of evaluating an artifact of this nature, it is still widely used on projects of similar scope as this one (e.g., Jabbarpour et al. (2014); Lisangan & Sumarta (2017); and Alsawy & Hefny (2010)).

In the following sections, different positions about using simulations for validation and the simulation setup for an instance of FAR are presented.

6.4.1   Validity in Simulation

With simulation, it is meant to build a likeliness; thus, the accuracy of such likeliness is a question that often rises (Kleindorfer et al., 1998). However, any method used for *validation* comes with a questionable satisfaction level and satisfactory level of defining that something is true or not.

From a philosophical perspective, an extreme objectivist would say that a model is valid or invalid and that the result is not open to interpretation. On the other hand, an extreme relativist would argue that a model validity is a matter of opinion (Kleindorfer et al., 1998). Both positions, however, are correct in a way; the objectivists try to find a standard frame to compare and evaluate models, so the process can transcend the model; the relativists attempt to find a common position between the model builders and the stakeholders contrarily.

Furthermore, most practitioners adopt an in-between position, meaning that they endorse the relevance of the empirical (i.e., scientific approach) without disregarding the communication with the stakeholders to establish a valid and credible model (Kleindorfer et al., 1998).

Thus, even when simulations are conducted under specific conditions and specific data, the author argues that their results provide good enough insights about the validity of the developed models and that they can be compared to the likes of the outcomes of other evaluation methods used in this context (i.e., case studies, controlled experiments, and field studies). Thus, by simulating scenarios, one can evaluate how an instance of the FAR framework will behave in an actual situation. Moreover, according to Barlas and Carpenter (1990), validation is "a matter of social conversion rather than objective confrontation," which supports the approach of making simulations to approximate how a model will behave in reality.

6.4.2   Simulation Setup

Defining a simulation setup is an arduous task, given that the last-mile delivery takes place under an environment that changes dynamically (e.g., traffic conditions and the presence of a customer at home).

However, as in previous research efforts (i.e., Jabbarpour et al. (2014); Lisangan & Sumarta (2017)), a set of factors can be defined toward setting up a close to reality, based-on-data environment.

For the goals of the FAR framework, a dataset depicting traffic conditions of specific areas within a city and the past delivery success for customers living within the selected area has to be available. Furthermore, the geographical area to be analyzed, the daypart, and parameters related to the FAS algorithm have to be specified.

The *geographical area* parameters are used to specify the surface in which the ants will move when finding the best route. These parameters are related to the geographical space that has to be covered. Table 6.1 presents them and the units in which they are specified.

The second parameter that has to be defined is the *daypart* when the simulation is going to be studied, namely morning, noon, afternoon, or evening. The value of this parameter is crucial given that it is used to select the traffic conditions to be taken into consideration and the delivery success for the customers.

Table 6.1 Parameters to be specified for the selection of the geographical area

Specification	Definition
Dimension	Measurement in kilometers of the area to be covered
Area	Area in square meters to be covered
Geohash	Geohash encoding of the selected area

Table 6.2 Parameters to be specified for the FAS algorithm and its ACO counterpart

Parameter	Definition
c	Number of cycles or iterations
m	Number of ants in the colony
ρ	Pheromone evaporation rate
α	Importance given to the trail pheromone intensity
β	Importance given to the visibility

The last set of parameters correspond to the ones related to the FAS algorithm. These parameters include the number of iterations c that the algorithm is going to be executed and the number of ants of the colony m (see Algorithm 6.1), whereas the parameters α, β, and τ are related to the weight or importance given to the visibility and pheromone intensity when selecting the next location (see Sect. 3.2.2). Table 6.2 summarizes and defines these parameters. It should be highlighted that the parameters α and β are defined only for the ACO counterpart of the FAS algorithm and that the other parameters are shared between the two approaches.

Once the parameters are defined, it is possible to compare the resulting routes provided by the FAR framework to similar algorithms such as the ACO and the A* algorithm (Hart et al., 1968). Furthermore, given that the ACO and the A* algorithm provide the best routes in terms of distance but not in terms of the highest rate of delivered parcels, a verification against a historical database of deliveries has to be performed to corroborate indeed that the FAR framework is providing the top-performing route to deliver the highest amount of packages in a specific part of the day. Moreover, the results obtained could be confirmed by experts in the field.

In regard to the implications for the implementation of an artifact, namely a prototype and its evaluation, special attention should be given to the data sources and their usage. The FAR framework pretends to approximate results without the need for precise information. Thus, when it comes to the traffic data, it should not come from the constant tracking of the location of vehicles that have not been authorized so and the same applies when studying the history of the past deliveries.

6.5 Further Readings

- **Van Duin et al. (2016).** "This research shows how to use historical delivery data to predict future delivery results by applying address intelligence. The application of multiple linear regression techniques supports the development of address intelligence identifying and predicting the improvement potential (rework) for other zip code areas" (abs.).

- **Jabbarpour et al. (2014).** "Finding a proper solution to vehicle congestion is a considerable challenge due to the dynamic and unpredictable nature of the network topology of vehicular environments, especially in urban areas. Instead of using static algorithms, e.g. Dijkstra and A*, we present a bio-inspired algorithm, food search behavior of ants, which is a promising way of solving traffic congestion in vehicular networks" (abs.).
- **Kleindorfer et al. (1998).** "There is still considerable doubt and even anxiety among simulation modelers as to what the methodologically correct guidelines or procedures for validating simulation models should be. The present paper attempts to give a description of the various philosophical positions as well as to summarize their problems and the kinds of evidentiary arguments they would each allow in arriving at defensible simulation models" (abs.).
- **Barlas and Carpenter (1990).** "System dynamics models, as causal models, are much like scientific theories. Hence, in evaluating such models, we assume certain norms of scientific inquiry. Most critics hold that the system dynamics approach does not employ formal, objective, quantitative model validation tests. This article argues that this type of criticism presupposes the traditional logical empiricist philosophy of science, which assumes that knowledge is an objective representation of reality and that theory justification can be an objective, formal proces" (abs.).

References

Alsawy, A.A. & Hefny, H.A. (2010). Fuzzy-based ant colony optimization algorithm. In *2010 2nd International Conference on Computer Technology and Development* (pp. 530–534). IEEE.

Barlas, Y. & Carpenter, S. (1990). Philosophical roots of model validation: two paradigms. *System Dynamics Review*, *6*, 148–166.

Hadorn, G.H., Biber-Klemm, S., Grossenbacher-Mansuy, W., Hoffmann-Riem, H., Joye, D., Pohl, C., Wiesmann, U. & Zemp, E. (2008). The emergence of transdisciplinarity as a form of research. In *Handbook of transdisciplinary research* (pp. 19–39). Springer.

Hart, P.E., Nilsson, N.J. & Raphael, B. (1968). A formal basis for the heuristic determination of minimum cost paths. *IEEE Transactions on Systems Science and Cybernetics*, *4*, 100–107.

Hevner, A.R., March, S.T., Park, J. & Ram, S. (2004). Design science in information systems research. *JSTOR*, 75–105.

Jabbarpour, M.R., Jalooli, A., Shaghaghi, E., Noor, R.M., Rothkrantz, L., Khokhar, R.H. & Anuar, N.B. (2014). Ant-based vehicle congestion avoidance system using vehicular networks. *Engineering Applications of Artificial Intelligence*, *36*, 303–319.

Kleindorfer, G.B., O'Neill, L. & Ganeshan, R. (1998). Validation in simulation: Various positions in the philosophy of science. *Management Science*, *44*, 1087–1099.

Kuechler, B. & Vaishnavi, V. (2008). On theory development in design science research: anatomy of a research project. *European Journal of Information Systems*, *17*, 489–504.

Lim, S.F.W., Jin, X. & Srai, J.S. (2018). Consumer-driven e-commerce. *International Journal of Physical Distribution & Logistics Management*.

Lisangan, E.A. & Sumarta, S.C. (2017). Route selection based on real time traffic condition using ant colony system and fuzzy inference system. In *2017 3rd International Conference on Science in Information Technology (ICSITech)* (pp. 66–71). IEEE.

Mańdziuk, J. (2018). New shades of the vehicle routing problem: emerging problem formulations and computational intelligence solution methods. *IEEE Transactions on Emerging Topics in Computational Intelligence, 3*, 230–244.

Mangiaracina, R., Perego, A., Seghezzi, A. & Tumino, A. (2019). Innovative solutions to increase last-mile delivery efficiency in b2c e-commerce: a literature review. *International Journal of Physical Distribution & Logistics Management.*

Pedrycz, W. (2020). *An introduction to computing with fuzzy sets: Analysis, design, and applications* (vol. 190). Springer Nature.

Pedrycz, W. & Wang, X. (2015). Designing fuzzy sets with the use of the parametric principle of justifiable granularity. *IEEE Transactions on Fuzzy Systems, 24*, 489–496.

Pincay, J., Portmann, E. & Terán, L. (2020b). Towards a computational intelligence framework to smartify the last-mile delivery. *POLIBITS, 62*, 85–91.

Teodorović, D. & Lučić, P. (2005). Schedule synchronization in public transit using the fuzzy ant system. *Transportation Planning and Technology, 28*, 47–76.

Teodorović, D. & Lučić, P. (2007). The fuzzy ant system for the vehicle routing problem when demand at nodes is uncertain. *International Journal on Artificial Intelligence Tools, 16*, 751–770.

Van Duin, J., De Goffau, W., Wiegmans, B., Tavasszy, L. & Saes, M. (2016). Improving home delivery efficiency by using principles of address intelligence for b2c deliveries. *Transportation Research Procedia, 12*, 14–25.

Chapter 7
The FAR Artifact

7.1 Architecture and Introduction to the Artifact

The development of this artifact takes as components the instantiations of the models described in Chaps. 4 and 5. Such implementations can be considered as pre-alpha stages of the overall prototype. As per the design science research principles, these implementations went through some iterations to produce an alpha version refined with the industrial partners participating in this research project.

The alpha versions allowed the author to produce a web-based prototype, using the implementations of Chaps. 4 and 5. For the sake of this work, the FAR artifact was implemented following a rapid approach that helps to demonstrate the concepts behind the FAR prototype and to evaluate it. Figure 7.1 illustrates the usage of the artifacts developed in this research work to formulate and implement the resulting FAR artifact; the arrows pointing out to the same artifact block indicate that they went through several iterations before obtaining the data needed for the implementation of the FAR artifact.

Figure 7.2 depicts the component architecture of the FAR artifact which lands in the practice the components of the FAR framework (see Fig. 6.1). Some of their specifications are:

- *Data Layer*: It is composed of three data sources. The first one is traffic probe data of delivery vehicles and records of their operations around the Bern area for July to November of 2018, and the second source corresponds to the traffic messages registered from 2018 to 2020. Even though these databases come from two different sources, they will be referred to as only one named DS_1, since the data were processed according to the methods described in Chap. 4. The third source corresponds to the history of deliveries of customers located in Bern from 2018 to 2020, with addresses within the postal codes 3011 and 3013. From now on, this data source is referred to as DS_2.

© The Author(s), under exclusive license to Springer Nature Switzerland AG 2022
J. Pincay Nieves, *Smart Urban Logistics*, Fuzzy Management Methods,
https://doi.org/10.1007/978-3-031-16704-1_7

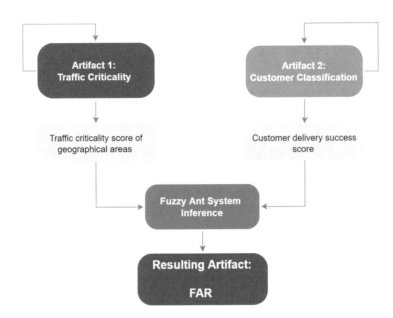

Fig. 7.1 Artifact usage in the formulation of the FAR artifact

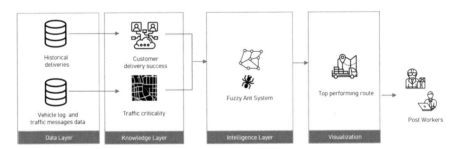

Fig. 7.2 FAR artifact architecture[*]
[*]All icons included are from the thenounproject.com used under Creative Commons license.

- *Knowledge Layer*: It contains the classifications of the customers according to the success of the past deliveries and areas of Bern scored according to their traffic criticality. It implements the process depicted previously in Fig. 6.2.
- *Intelligence Layer:* It implements the FAS algorithm (see Algorithm 6.1) using the data of the knowledge layer and produces the top-performing route to deliver the highest number of parcels in one tour.
- *Visualization Layer:* This is a web-based interface that uses a map to display the outcome of the Intelligence Layer to the users.

Furthermore, the logic of the artifact was implemented with Python and the framework Django was used to build a functional web application to display the results. The library Simpful (Spolaor et al., 2020) was used to define the linguistic variables, the fuzzy inference system, and perform the inferences. Finally, the library Folium was used to create the maps.

In the following sections, detailed information about the implementation of the components of the prototype is provided.

7.1.1 Data Sources Description

To implement the FAR artifact, the data sources of the applications described in Chaps. 4 and 5 were used. Furthermore, a similar cleaning process was applied. Specific aspects about the data sources and the data selection used in the implementation of the FAR artifact are presented next.

7.1.1.1 Probe Data of Delivery Vehicles and Traffic Messages

The data source DS_1 was composed of two databases, which were the same used in the development described in Chap. 4. The two databases are:

1. $DS_{1.1}$—*Probe data:* GPS data of six months of operations of logistic vehicles of a postal company based in Switzerland. The records contained information on the location of the vehicles during their delivery operations; among them are mileage, speed, events (e.g., parked, motor on, and motor off), and postal code. Only data points of the area of Bern were considered.
2. $DS_{1.2}$—*Traffic Message Channel-based records:* Traffic messages delivered through the Traffic Message Channel (TMC) technology (Gao & Wen, 2007) and processed by *Viasuisse*, during the years 2018 to 2020. These messages are generated by the traffic monitoring responsible (i.e., police officers and municipalities), and they record incidents varying from traffic anomalies, road accidents to road works and events (e.g., parades, concerts, and demonstrations) that cause traffic delays.

The details about the data structures of both databases are presented in Appendix A (see Tables A.1, A.2).

After the data cleaning process, the $DS_{1.1}$ was composed of about 315,014 sampling points, and each record was described in terms of 14 fields among which there were position, timestamps, distance, non-traffic vehicular related information, and events depicting internal vehicular state such as power on/off, ignition, movement, and waiting. Once the selection, segmentation, and calculation of the segment speed were made, the final database had 34,470 records which contained timestamp information, deduced speed, and the GPS coordinates encoded with geohashes of level 7 (i.e., bounding boxes of 153 m × 153 m).

Regarding the $DS_{1.2}$, once the cleaning, selection, and augmentation steps were completed, it was formed by 5013 records and 15 fields, including timestamps of the start and end of the event, coordinates, and names of the start and end locations,

Table 7.1 Sample of the
records of the DS_1 used in
the implementations of the
FAR artifact

Geohash	Traffic criticality	Timestamp
u0m71dt	0.6997	2018-03-26 11:10:00
u0m71de	0.3512	2018-04-07 16:40:00
u0m716e	0.0778	2018-05-04 06:40:00

duration, and description of the event. These records contained additional fields depicting the time of the day and the coordinates where the incident happened encoded with level 7 geohashes.

Furthermore, the two datasets are processed following the schema presented in Chap. 4 to produce the dataset with the traffic criticality score, which indicates how critical is the traffic in a particular area on a scale of 0 to 1, with 0, meaning that the traffic in one area is not critical at a specific time, and 1 that is highly critical.

Table 7.1 shows some example records of the DS_1 used for the FAR artifact implementation; the fields depict the geographical coordinates of the records encoded in geohash, the traffic score, and the timestamp when the score was computed.

7.1.1.2   History of Deliveries to Customers

This dataset was provided by *Swiss Post*, one of the data partners in developing this work. This dataset (DS_2) is the same used in developing the application described in Chap. 5. It contained information about different deliveries in the city of Bern that took place during the years 2018, 2019, and half of 2020. For this study, the postal codes 3011 and 3013 were taken into consideration.

In total, there were 7,016,584 events in the initial dataset. Fourteen attributes describe every event. After a careful examination, attributes containing information regarding the type of customer (i.e., natural or legal), street, house number, type of the event (e.g., delivered or not delivered), the way the delivery took place (e.g., given to the customer, left by the mailbox or by the door), and the date were taken into account. Records with missing or duplicated information were neglected. Only the ones targeted to natural persons (and not legal or companies) were kept; this consideration was taken since from the data, it was confirmed that deliveries to companies are more successful as they almost always have people around.

Furthermore, it was also necessary to define what a successful and what an unsuccessful delivery is, taking into consideration the information from the dataset: a *successful delivery* is a delivery that was handed directly to the customer at home, and an *unsuccessful delivery* is a delivery that was not handed directly to the customer at home or is not delivered at all.

After this stage, DS_2 consisted of 453,076 deliveries to natural persons. Furthermore, for the implementation of the prototype, only spring months (March, April, and May) were considered, resulting in 1786 customers and 30,675 deliveries.

Table 7.2 Sample of the records of the DS_2 used in the implementations of the FAR artifact

ID	Latitude	Longitude	Geohash	Monday morning	Tuesday afternoon
7,010,002	46.94851	7.456	u0m71dt	0.0	0.0139
7,010,058	46.94857	7.4565	u0m71de	0.4	0.38
7,064,161	46.94810	7.442	u0m716e	0.166	0.275

Finally, a score that indicates the success of the delivery for the customers during the morning for every weekday was computed (see Sect. 5.4). The score is a value between 0 and 1, where 0 means that a delivery always fails and 1 that the historical deliveries were always successful. Also, the geographical coordinates of the customers' locations were encoded with geohashes of level 7 to ease the data processing.

Table 7.2 shows some example records of the DS_2 used for the FAR artifact implementation with 6 out of the 31 fields. The other fields correspond to the address and the score for the other weekdays' dayparts.

7.1.2   Traffic Criticality

Recalling the process for the Knowledge Layer illustrated in Fig. 6.2, the following steps were performed toward extracting the required knowledge from DS_1 to feed the Intelligence Layer.

- *Data Selection:* For the implementation, only the records of DS_1 that corresponded to the spring months (March, April, and May) of the years 2018 and 2019 were selected. A further filter corresponded to the selection of the records that had time between 07h00 and 10h00 (morning). Furthermore, given that for a certain area, there are traffic criticality scores for different times; these are grouped and the median of all the scores computed. The median was chosen since, in the literature, it has been shown that it performs better in terms of accuracy than other measures such as the mean (Lisangan & Sumarta, 2017; Salehinejad & Talebi, 2010).
- *Data Partition and Linguistic Variable Definition:* With the selected data, the parametric principle of justifiable granularity was applied to form meaningful information granules (data partition). As a result, the linguistic variable *traffic criticality* was defined, with a universe of discourse [0, 1], and divided into four fuzzy sets with the linguistic labels: *not critical*, *low critical*, *critical*, and *highly critical*.

  The fuzzy sets corresponding to the labels obtained from the dataset described in the previous point are presented in Fig. 7.3.

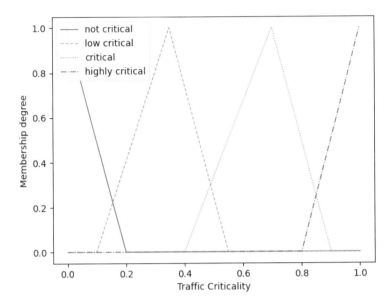

Fig. 7.3 Terms of the linguistic variable *traffic criticality* over the domain [0,1]

7.1.3 Customer Delivery Success

Similarly to for the *traffic criticality*, the Knowledge Layer process over the DB_2 consisted of the following:

- *Data Selection:* The delivery success score for the customers living within the areas represented with the postal codes 3011 and 3013 was selected. As in the DS_1, only data stamped with dates corresponding to spring months and 2018 to 2019 were selected. A further filter corresponded to selecting only the scores corresponding to the mornings of the weekdays.
- *Data Partition and Linguistic Variable Definition:* The parametric principle of justifiable granularity was applied once again over the filtered data. As outcome, it was possible to define the linguistic variable *delivery success* with a universe of discourse [0, 1] and divided into four fuzzy sets with the linguistic labels: *always unsuccessful, sometimes successful, frequently successful,* and *always successful.*

  The fuzzy sets corresponding to the aforementioned linguistic labels are depicted in Fig. 7.4. Furthermore, it was verified that the definition of the linguistic variable met the design criteria and constraints defined in Sect. 3.1.5.

Additionally, since there are four linguistic variables (i.e., *traffic criticality, delivery success, distance,* and *pheromone intensity*) that need to be taken into consideration when determining the utility of the next node for the ants, the number of linguistic labels was set to 4 (for this case and in the case of the *traffic criticality*).

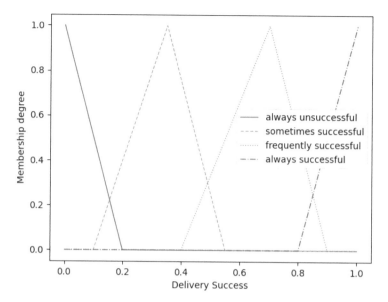

Fig. 7.4 Terms of the linguistic variable *delivery success* over the domain [0,1]

This design choice was taken to avoid an explosion on the number of fuzzy rules that the Intelligence Layer has to implement.

7.1.4 FAS Algorithm Implementation

As previously stated, the logic of the FAS algorithm was implemented with Python. The details specific to the implementation are presented next.

7.1.4.1 Encoding Geospatial Information with Geohashes

As presented in Chap. 4, geohash indexing proved to be a helpful manner to aggregate and study geospatial data to study traffic. The indexing with geohash was used in the implementation of FAS algorithm; they represent the nodes that the ants have to visit. The goal of this procedure was that each geohash contains information about the traffic criticality of an area and, for a customer, it is also possible to encode information about its address.

In this way, it is feasible to obtain information about the traffic, a particular customer household location, and to compute the distance between them with the same identifier (i.e., a geohash). Thus, the FAS algorithm problem is reduced to finding the best route between geohashes. Figure 7.5 illustrates this concept.

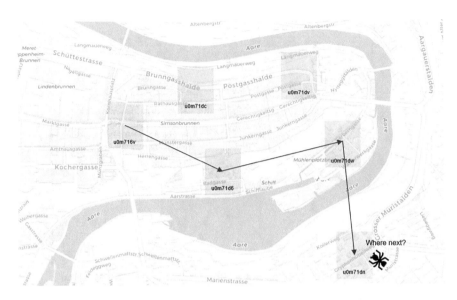

Fig. 7.5 Usage of geohashes to simplify the implementation of the FAS algorithm

Table 7.3 Sample of the records of the DS_1 and DS_2 merged on the geohash field

ID	Latitude	Longitude	Geohash	Monday morning	Tuesday afternoon	Traffic criticality
7,010,002	46.94851	7.456	u0m71dt	0.0	0.0139	0.6997
7,010,058	46.94857	7.4565	u0m71de	0.4	0.38	0.3512
7,064,161	46.94810	7.442	u0m716e	0.166	0.275	0.0778

The usefulness of performing this indexing method can be further understood by examining Table 7.3 presented in the coming section.

7.1.4.2   Data for Traffic and Customer Delivery

Sections 7.1.2 and 7.1.3 characterized the datasets for the traffic criticality and the customer historic deliveries. One further step that was performed to make the FAS algorithm work was to merge both datasets on the geohash field.

In this way, the geohashes are treated as *nodes* to locate the ants and to build the routes. The geohashes will therefore contain the traffic criticality and the morning delivery success for each customer. Recalling the examples of records of Tables 7.1 and 7.2, the merged dataset will look similar to the entries presented in Table 7.3; for space constraint, only the main fields are shown.

7.1.4.3 Distance and Pheromone Intensity

The distance between delivery locations has to be computed. Thus, the linguistic variables defining it and the pheromone intensity are to be defined as well.

For the distance, as the studied geographical area of the postal codes, 3011 and 3013, is approximately 3 km^2, the universe of discourse was chosen between 0 and 5 (kilometers). Since the pheromone intensity is a value between 0 and 1, the same range was chosen as the universe of discourse.

Furthermore, aiming to reduce the number of possible combinations for fuzzy rules needed for the reasoning algorithm, for both cases, only three linguistic labels were defined. For the linguistic variable *distance*, the linguistic labels are *small*, *medium*, and *long*; in the case of the linguistic variable pheromone intensity, the linguistic labels are *weak*, *medium*, and *strong*.

The fuzzy sets corresponding to the abovementioned linguistic labels for both variables are depicted in Fig. 7.6. Furthermore, it was verified that the definition of the linguistic variables met the design criteria and constraints defined in Sect. 3.1.5.

7.1.4.4 Fuzzy Rules Reasoning

With all the linguistic variables defined, before implementing the FAS algorithm, it was necessary to define the fuzzy rule basis considering all the possible values of the previously defined linguistic variables.

For the fuzzy rule reasoning, the linguistic variables *traffic criticality*, *delivery success*, *distance*, and *pheromone intensity* constitute the antecedents. As per the explanations presented in Sect. 6.3.3, the consequent of the rules is the concept of *utility*, which is the preference of an ant to choose the next link.

In a similar fashion as for the antecedents, the *utility* was modeled as a linguistic variable. Since this is a value between 0 and 1, the interval [0, 1] was chosen as the universe of discourse with the linguistic labels *very low utility (VLU)*, *low utility (LU)*, *medium utility (MU)*, *high utility (HU)*, and *very high utility (VHU)*.

The fuzzy sets corresponding to the linguistic labels for the variable utility for both variables are presented in Fig. 7.7. Furthermore, it was verified that the definition of the linguistic variable met the design criteria and constraints defined in Sect. 3.1.5.

With the antecedents and the consequent defined, it was possible to define the basis for the rule-based reasoning. In total, 144 rules were characterized. For example, when choosing the next location, the ones with *small* distances, *strong* pheromone intensity, with a customer whose deliveries are *frequently successful*, and with *low traffic criticality* have a *very high utility*. On the contrary, when the distances are *long*, the pheromone intensity is *weak*, the deliveries are *frequently unsuccessful*, and with *critical* traffic, the utility is estimated to be *very low*. Moreover, it should be highlighted that the consequent is determined using the Sugeno inference model (see Sect. 3.1.4); in this way, the defuzzification process is avoided, and thus, the computation times are reduced.

A sample of the implemented fuzzy rules is presented in Table 7.4.

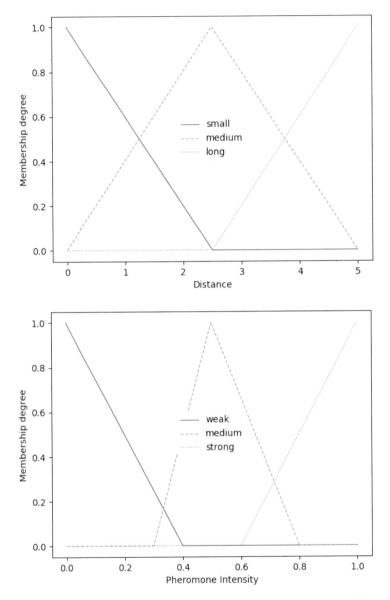

Fig. 7.6 Terms of the linguistic variable *distance* over the domain [0,5] (top) and of the variable *pheromone intensity* over the domain [0,1] (bottom)

Furthermore, the parameters of the FAS algorithm (see Table 6.2) were tuned and set accordingly to some recommendations in the literature (Tatomir & Rothkrantz, 2006; Teodorović & Lučić, 2005). Table 7.5 presents the values used for the implementation of the FAR prototype.

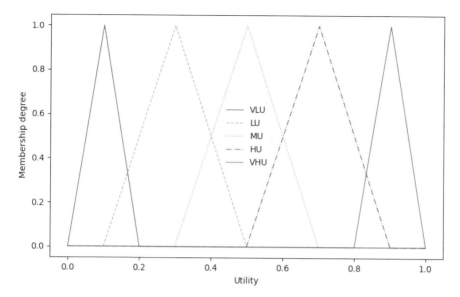

Fig. 7.7 Terms of the linguistic variable *utility* over the domain [0,1]

Table 7.4 Selection of fuzzy rules implemented for FAR artifact

	IF				THEN
Rule	Distance	Pheromone intensity	Delivery success	Traffic criticality	Utility
1	Small	Weak	Always unsuccessful	Critical	VLU
2	Small	Weak	Sometimes successful	Highly critical	LU
3	Small	Weak	Frequently successful	Not critical	MU
4	Small	Medium	Frequently successful	Low critical	HU
5	Small	Strong	Frequently successful	Not critical	VHU
6	Medium	Weak	Always unsuccessful	Highly critical	VLU
7	Medium	Weak	Sometimes successful	Critical	LU
8	Medium	Medium	Frequently successful	Critical	LU
9	Long	Strong	Always successful	Not critical	HU
10	Long	Strong	Frequently successful	Critical	LU

Table 7.5 Parameters of FAS algorithm for the FAR prototype and its ACO counterpart

Parameter	Value
c	50
m	25
ρ	0.5
α (For ACO only)	1.0
β (For ACO only)	0.5

7.1.4.5 Verification of the Design Criteria for Fuzzy Rules

Section 3.1.5.3 presented a set of criteria that have to be considered when defining fuzzy rules. The implementation of the FAR artifact implied verifying the accomplishment of those criteria:

(i) *Rule length:* This rule states that the number of fuzzy rules should be as small as possible. This criterion was hard to meet given that the four variables constitute the antecedents of the rules, and each of them has 3 to 4 linguistic labels.

   Thus, as suggested by Hudec (2016), as a way of addressing this problem (curse of dimensionality), the rules that contained in the antecedent that the delivery is *always unsuccessful* for a customer were removed. This decision was taken because the consequent for those rules will have as consequent *VLU*. In this way, the number of effective rules used for the inference is reduced to 108 (from 144) rules, and thus the criterion is partially met.

(ii) *Local models:* The rules were designed in a way that the consequents represent a direct effect of all the antecedents in a way that they can be understood. Hence, this criterion follows the local models constraint definition.

(iii) *Granular consequents:* The outputs of all the rules are represented by linguistic terms. Thus, this criterion is accomplished.

7.1.4.6 Python Implementation

The previously described linguistic variables and rules were implemented with Python. With the library Simpful, the process was significantly simplified as only a few lines of code are needed to implement a working fuzzy inference system. For instance, the declaration of the fuzzy system and the implementation of the linguistic variable *traffic criticality* are presented in Listing 7.1. The other linguistic variables were declared similarly.

Listing 7.1 Python implementation of the linguistic variable *traffic criticality*

```
FS = FuzzySystem()
T_1 = FuzzySet(function=Triangular_MF(a=0, b=0, c=0.2),
               term="not_critical")
T_2 = FuzzySet(function=Triangular_MF(a=0.1, b=0.35, c=0.55),
               term="low_critical")
T_3 = FuzzySet(function=Triangular_MF(a=0.4, b=0.7, c=0.9),
               term="critical")
T_4 = FuzzySet(function=Triangular_MF(a=0.8, b=1),
               term="highly_critical")
lv4 = LinguisticVariable([T_1, T_2, T_3, T_4],
                         concept="Traffic_Criticality",
                         universe_of_discourse=[0, 1])
FS.add_linguistic_variable("TrafficCriticality", lv4)
```

Once all linguistic variables were defined, it was possible to declare the fuzzy rules. The 108 fuzzy rules were declared as variables and then added to the fuzzy system. Listing 7.2 depicts an example of the declaration of two of the fuzzy rules used for the FAR prototype.

Listing 7.2 Python implementation of two fuzzy rules of the FAR prototype

```
1    R62 = "IF (Distance IS medium) AND (PheromoneIntensity IS
     weak) AND (DeliverySuccess IS  always_successful) AND (
     TrafficCriticality IS low_critical) THEN (Utility IS MU)"
2    R99 = "IF (Distance IS long) AND (PheromoneIntensity IS weak)
      AND (DeliverySuccess IS  always_successful) AND (
     TrafficCriticality IS not_critical) THEN (Utility IS MU)"
```

Furthermore, the code used for the implementation of Algorithm 6.1 can be found in Appendix D.

Nevertheless, given the high number of rules, the execution times were high too; thus, the implementation decision of not considering for the routing those customers which are known that the delivery is going to fail (i.e., the *delivery success* is *always unsuccessful* for a certain daypart) was taken, as explained previously. The interface informs about those customers, so they can be allocated at some other delivery daypart.

7.1.5   Web Interface

The Python framework for web development Django was used to develop an interface that has the goal of displaying the output of the FAS algorithm. Such an interface corresponds to the implementation of the Visualization Layer of the FAR framework.

As it was explained in the previous section, the Python implementation of the FAS algorithm provides the top-performing route to deliver the highest amount of parcels. Additionally, it also displays the customers that need to be allocated in another time frame since the deliveries will be approximately always unsuccessful on a specific time window.

Both pieces of information are shown to the user. On a map, the order in which the route should be completed is displayed, and on the bottom the data of the customers whose deliveries are more convenient to be completed at another time and a suggestion of when this should be done. Figure 7.8 shows an instance of the interface of the FAR artifact.

Fuzzy Ant Routing - FAR

Fig. 7.8 Web interface of the FAR artifact

Table 7.6 Parameters of the selected geographical area for the evaluation of the FAR artifact

Specification	Value
Dimension	≈ 2.45 km $\times 1.22$ km
Area	≈ 3 km^2
Geohashes	$u0m717$, $u9m71e$, $u0m718$, and $u0m71s$

7.2 Evaluation

This section presents the results of the simulations performed to evaluate the utility, quality, and efficacy of the FAR framework. The simulations were completed according to the specifications detailed in Sect. 6.4.

The simulations were executed using a computer with an Intel Core i7 @ 1.10 GHz processor, 32 GB of memory RAM, and `Python` 3.7 environment.

Regarding the geographical area selected for the simulations, it corresponded to the postal codes 3011 and 3013 of the city of Bern. Further details are presented in Table 7.6.

In terms of the time window of analysis, only the morning over weekdays, excluding the weekends (Saturday and Sunday) of the spring months of 2018 and 2019, were studied. Furthermore, the outcome of the delivery route was compared to what happened on a randomly selected spring day of the year 2020.

For the FAS parameters, the ones specified previously in Table 7.5 were implemented.

In total, four simulations to obtain a delivery route were completed. The number of customers varied from 5 to 50. The results of the FAS artifact were compared to an implementation of an ACO algorithm (Dorigo & Di Caro, 1999) and an A* algorithm implementation (Hart et al., 1968). The ACO and A* implementations were used to create the routes from the available data as the actual routes used were not provided by the data partners. Furthermore, the implementation of the A* algorithm available from the `Python` library `mlrose` was used for the sake of the evaluation stage, whereas the ACO algorithm was programmed by the author.

The results of the simulation for 5, 10, and 15 customers are presented in Table 7.7, whereas the results for 50 customers are shown in Table 7.8. The customers were selected randomly as well as the days to analyze. However, it was verified that the selected customers registered deliveries for the specific days that were used to determine the percentage of successful deliveries. The percentage of successful deliveries was computed by counting the number of customers that received a package in their hands on a randomly selected day and dividing that result by the total number of deliveries to be performed that day.

The percentage of successful deliveries for the ACO and the A* algorithm is comparable to what happened during the delivery process in 2020, whereas the result for the FAR artifact is the outcome of considering also the recommendations of deliveries on the other dayparts for the computation.

From the results presented in Tables 7.7 and 7.8, it can be observed that the FAR artifact performs better than the route resulting of the ACO and the A* algorithms in terms of the delivery success. Although the outcome for FAR may seem low, compared to the actual events, it provides promising results, recalling that the percentage of successful deliveries for natural customers on average is around 30% (see Chap. 5).

Regarding the tour length, it is shorter for the case of FAR than for ACO and A* which was expected given that both algorithms find the best performing routes considering the distances between locations, and because in the case of FAR, fewer locations are to be visited during the studied daypart. Figure 7.9 (left) depicts the aforementioned; it can be observed that the difference tends to remain proportional to the number of customers to visit. When it comes to the execution times, the results are not that favorable for FAR as they are higher than the ones of ACO and also to A* (see Fig. 7.9 (right)). This is derived from the fact that further computations and inferences have to be performed when getting the performing routes through FAR. The execution time of FAR can be approximated to the order $O(n)$ whereas for ACO and A* to $O(log_2 n)$.

Furthermore, Fig. 7.10 summarizes the findings after the evaluation process in the form of a SWOT analysis of FAR and also evaluated algorithms ACO and A*.

Table 7.7 Comparison of the results of the simulation to determine a delivery route for 5, 10, and 15 customers

Day/ daypart	Number of customers	Method Method	Route recommendation	% of successful deliveries	Tour length (km)	Execution time (sec)
Monday morning	5	FAR	7010176-7010212-7010753-7010130	52%	1.92	2.02
			Wednesday morning: 7010002			
		ACO	7010176-7010212-7010002-7010753-7010130	25%	2.00	0.19
		A*	7010176-7010212-7010753-010130-7010002	25%	1.98	0.68
Tuesday morning	10	FAR	7010045-7010130-7010664-7010277-7010176-7010002	70%	2.01	5.39
			Monday morning: 7010753, 7010282			
			Friday morning: 7010212, 7010064			
		ACO	7010130-7010664-7010753-7010045-7010064-7010002-7010277-7010282-7010212-7010176	39%	3.35	0.26
		A*	7010212-7010212-7010176-7010002-7010064-7010045-7010664-7010753-7010277-7010282	39%	3.18	0.74
Monday morning	15	FAR	7010753-7010282-7010175-7010179-7010212-7010176-7010234-7010277-7010664-7010606-7011012-7010130	61%	2.05	26.65
			Tuesday morning: 7010045			
			Wednesday morning: 7010002			
			Thursday morning: 7010064			

(continued)

Table 7.7 (continued)

Day/ daypart	Number of customers	Method Method	Route recommendation	% of successful deliveries	Tour length (km)	Execution time (sec)
		ACO	7010130-7010664-7010606-7011012-7010753-7010045-7010064-7010002-7010277-7010282-7010212-7010175-7010179-7010176-7010234	30%	2.44	0.35
		A*	7010175-7010234-7010179-7010002-7010176-7010664-7010606-7011012-7010045-7010282-7010212-7010212-7010277-7010753-7010064	30%	2.41	2.85

7.3 Analysis of Results and Lessons Learned

The concepts and ideas developed along this book were applied and integrated into the FAR conceptual framework. This framework served as the footprint to implement a working prototype that enables finding the top-performing route to deliver packages for the last mile, considering aspects such as traffic criticality, history of past deliveries, and distance between locations, and using FAS principles. Fuzzy logic was the primary tool to model and handle the uncertainty and lack of precise information of the concepts mentioned above. It also enabled using swarm intelligence under these conditions.

With the artifact, it was also possible to verify the advantages of using swarm intelligence. The resulting prototype was robust, meaning that the task could be completed even if some agents (ants) fail; it was scalable and adaptable since the number of ants and nodes can be increased or reduced easily, and it was decentralized because there is no central control in the colony, and thus a network can be fully explored.

The results of the implementation of the FAR artifact and the simulations meet the objectives of this research effort. It was possible to create a delivery tour, while respecting the customer's privacy and with traffic data that does not come from the constant tracking of users using mobile devices or from devices deployed in large areas. The usage of geohash indexing allowed the author to include an additional layer of data protection (for the customer addresses) and to ease the implementation of the prototype since the data could be processed and aggregated straightforwardly and represent the locations to be visited.

Table 7.8 Comparison of the results of the simulation to determine a delivery route for 50 customers

Day daypart	Number of customers	Method Method	Route recommendation	% of successful deliveries	Tour length (km)	Execution time (sec)
Friday morning	50	FAR	7010010-7010063-7010065-7010178-7010231-7010082-7010173-710252-7010263-7010218-7010283-7010277-7010219-7010289-7010285-7010172-7010175-7010085-7010233-7010234-7010176-7010066-7010191-7010224-7010232-7010053-7010044-7010062-7010105-7010113-7010117-7010217-7010267-7010040	68%	4.21	267.42
			Monday morning: 7010012-7010087-7010119-7010127-7010157			
			Tuesday morning: 7010045-7010130-7010167-7010261			
			Wednesday morning: 7010002-7010041-7010269			
			Thursday morning: 7010064-7010158-7010164-7010274			
		ACO	7010176-7010178-7010065-7010066-7010175-7010172-7010224-7010173-7010234-7010191-7010167-7010082-7010233-7010232-7010085-7010087-7010105-7010127-7010113-7010231-7010117-7010119-7010217-7010274-7010219-7010002-7010218-7010010-			

(continued)

Table 7.8 (continued)

Day daypart	Number of customers	Method Method	Route recommendation	% of successful deliveries	Tour length (km)	Execution time (sec)
			7010064-7010012-710252-7010277-7010283-7010285-7010289-7010261-7010040-7010263-7010044-7010063-7010269-7010267-7010041-7010045-7010053-7010062-7010157-7010158-7010164-7010130	42%	5.50	2.01
		A*	7010130-7010164-7010045-7010010-7010040-7010085-7010191-7010267-7010217-7010175-7010082-7010219-7010261-7010053-7010041-7010269-7010173-7010063-7010002-7010012-7010064-710105-7010066-7010285-7010087-7010218-7010224-7010277-7010263-7010127-7010119-7010117-7010234-7010176-7010167-7010113-7010065-7010274-7010232-7010178-7010172-7010283-7010231-7010289-7010158-710157-7010233-7010044-7010062-710252-	42%	9.66	2.11

It was verified that the obtained routes for the simulations are feasible to be completed. There is, however, one feature that needs to be evaluated against the business rules and preferences of the customers. The FAR prototype proposes alternative delivery days when the customer is most likely to receive a package; this means that the parcel is delivered later than expected. Per information received from a data partner, when the customer is not at home, they get an invitation to go to a postal office and fetch the package within ten days. Thus, a more refined implementation must define the business rules and preferences of the customers to

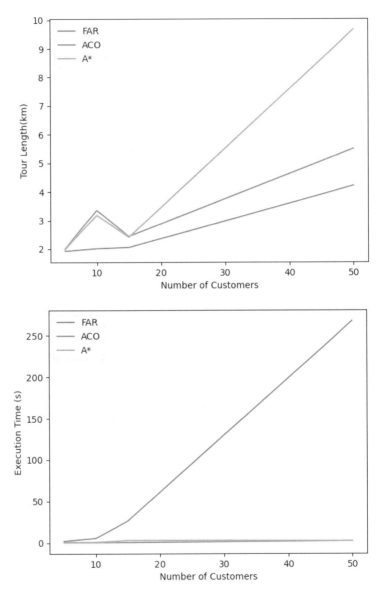

Fig. 7.9 Plot of results of the tour length for a number of customers for FAR and ACO (left) and of the execution times (right)

decide if the parcel is delivered during the suggested daypart or if the delivery staff must proceed as defined by the company's politics.

Nevertheless, it should be highlighted that since the conception of the design of the FAR framework, the law of parsimony was followed, and the resulting artifact is closer to a mockup than to an end product. Some aspects are yet to be considered

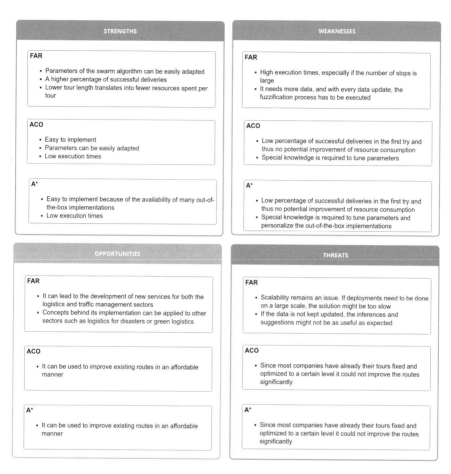

Fig. 7.10 SWOT analysis of FAR, ACO, and A* after the evaluation stage

and further analyzed for the FAR prototype to be a fully functional product. One of them is related to the execution times of the implementation. The results presented tend to increment linearly with the number of customers to be visited. This can be inconvenient when the solution needs to be deployed at a larger scale. Thus, the interests of a delivery company need to come into play and decide whether a possible increase in customer satisfaction and the development of a new project that might be another source of income is enough to invest in the infrastructure for the deployment of a project of this nature. Also, depending on the business rules, the number of rules to perform the inferences when selecting the following location to visit could be reduced, which may eventually reduce the running times of the algorithm.

Those above, however, would not be a critical point if the conceptions of the FAR framework are used to implement products in other domains such as logistics of heavy transportation, tourism, or emergency services. This is stated considering that in such domains, the number of customers and the number of locations to visit are smaller, and the FAR framework allows implementing solutions of such nature.

Another aspect of being considered is that although simulations offer a good overview of how an implementation will work in the real world, the FAR artifact has yet to be evaluated in an actual use case. Aspects such as traffic and the presence of a person at home can be approximated as presented in this research work, but sudden events could completely change patterns and models. A clear example is the Covid-19 global pandemic. It directly influenced the aspects studied in this work (traffic on the streets and presence of a person at home). Thus, a possible way of addressing issues such as this one is keeping the available data updated and thus updating the concepts depicted by the linguistic variables and the corresponding fuzzy sets.

7.4   Further Readings

- **Spolaor et al. (2020).** "In this work we propose Simpful, a general-purpose and user-friendly Python library designed to facilitate the definition, analysis, and interpretation of fuzzy inference systems. Simpful provides a lightweight Application Programming Interface that allows to intuitively define fuzzy sets and fuzzy rules, and to perform fuzzy inference" (abs.).
- **Xiang (2019).** "With the rapid development of location-aware mobile devices, location-based services have been widely used. When LBS (Location Based Services) bringing great convenience and profits, it also brings great hidden trouble, among which user privacy security is one of them. The paper builds a LBS privacy protection model and develops algorithm depend on the technology of one dimensional coding of geohash geographic information" (abs.).
- **Salehinejad and Talebi (2010).** "This paper introduces a multiparameter route selection system which employs fuzzy logic (FL) for local pheromone updating of an ant colony system (ACS) in detection of optimum multiparameter direction between two desired points, origin and destination (O/D)" (abs.).

References

Dorigo, M. & Di Caro, G. (1999). Ant colony optimization: a new meta-heuristic. In *Proceedings of the 1999 congress on evolutionary computation-CEC99 (Cat. No. 99TH8406)* (vol. 2, 1470–1477). IEEE.

Gao, Y. & Wen, H.m. (2007). Technique and standardization research of radio data system-traffic message channel (rds-tmc). *Journal of Transportation Systems Engineering and Information Technology, 3*.

Hart, P.E., Nilsson, N.J. & Raphael, B. (1968). A formal basis for the heuristic determination of minimum cost paths. *IEEE transactions on Systems Science and Cybernetics, 4*, 100–107.

Hudec, M. (2016). *Fuzziness in information systems* (pp. 67–99). Springer International Publishing.

Jaha, A., Jaha, D., Pincay, J., TerÁn, L. & Portmann, E. (2021). Privacy-friendly delivery plan recommender. In *2021 Eighth International Conference on eDemocracy eGovernment (ICEDEG)* (pp. 146–151).

Lisangan, E.A. & Sumarta, S.C. (2017). Route selection based on real time traffic condition using ant colony system and fuzzy inference system. In *2017 3rd International Conference on Science in Information Technology (ICSITech)* (pp. 66–71). IEEE.

Pincay, J., Mensah, A.O., Portmann, E. & Terán, L. (2020a). Partitioning space to identify en-route movement patterns. In *2020 Seventh International Conference on eDemocracy & eGovernment (ICEDEG)* (pp. 43–49). IEEE.

Pincay, J., Portmann, E. & TerÁn, L. (2021a). Fuzzifying geospatial data to identify critical traffic areas. In *Joint Proceedings of the 19th World Congress of the International Fuzzy Systems Association (IFSA), the 12th Conference of the European Society for Fuzzy Logic and Technology (EUSFLAT), and the 11th International Summer School on Aggregation Operators (AGOP)* (pp. 463–470). Atlantis Press.

Salehinejad, H. & Talebi, S. (2010). Dynamic fuzzy logic-ant colony system-based route selection system. *Applied Computational Intelligence and Soft Computing*, 2010.

Spolaor, S., Fuchs, C., Cazzaniga, P., Kaymak, U., Besozzi, D. & Nobile, M.S. (2020). Simpful: A user-friendly python library for fuzzy logic. *International Journal of Computational Intelligence Systems*, **13**, 1687–1698.

Tatomir, B. & Rothkrantz, L. (2006). Hierarchical routing in traffic using swarm-intelligence. In *2006 IEEE Intelligent Transportation Systems Conference* (pp. 230–235). IEEE.

Teodorović, D. & Lučić, P. (2005). Schedule synchronization in public transit using the fuzzy ant system. *Transportation Planning and Technology*, **28**, 47–76.

Xiang, W. (2019). An efficient location privacy preserving model based on geohash. In *2019 6th International Conference on Behavioral, Economic and Socio-Cultural Computing (BESC)* (pp. 1–5). IEEE.

Part V
Conclusions

Chapter 8
Outlook and Conclusions

8.1 Summary

Mobility is vital for the development of cities and the well-being of their citizens. It influences multiple sectors, from the economy to services. Even if attempting to perform improvements might be challenging given the many actors and perspectives involved, still, efforts should be invested to ameliorate any of its aspects.

In this work, it was chosen to address issues of the logistics and services aspect of mobility, precisely, the last-mile delivery. To that effect, data coming from logistic trucks were used to create traffic analysis models; likewise, the history of past deliveries to customers was studied to perform a privacy-friendly classification according to how likely it is that someone is at home when a delivery person rings the bell. To achieve such a goal, the design science methodology was applied in combination with a transdisciplinary approach. With the design science guidelines, several artifacts were implemented from where it was possible to learn aspects about traffic and customers' presence at home. Following the transdisciplinary approach, the author was able to work with industrial practitioners from the postal service (Swiss Post) and traffic management (Viasuisse) sectors. Their practical know-how was included in the development of the solutions and their evaluation. As an outcome, a framework that enables an improved first-try delivery ratio for the last-mile delivery was proposed.

In developing the framework mentioned above, it was first necessary to be familiar with the concepts of Smart Cities and Human-Smart City. It was also imperative to understand the logistic services' main problems when using the city's streets and roads; both aspects were studied in Chap. 2.

Once the last-mile delivery problems were recognized, the next step consisted of exploring the theories that enable addressing the challenges of working with incomplete and inaccurate geospatial traffic data. Furthermore, methods that allow classifying postal customers respecting their privacy were also studied. Finally, finding ways of creating new routes considering the traffic and customers' presence

J. Pincay Nieves, *Smart Urban Logistics*, Fuzzy Management Methods,
https://doi.org/10.1007/978-3-031-16704-1_8

at home was also needed. The exploration and selection of such methods were performed in Chap. 3.

With the problems defined and the suitable theories that can be applied to find a solution for them identified, the development of artifacts that enabled conveying information from geospatial traffic data and classifying customers in a privacy-friendly manner took place. The details about the development of these artifacts were presented in Chaps. 4 and 5.

Thanks to the knowledge obtained from the development of the artifacts and by exchanging with the industry partners in the process, it was possible to define the FAR conceptual framework in Chap. 6. The FAR framework aimed to create routes to improve the first-try ratio of the last-mile delivery; it is composed of four different layers, having as the core the Knowledge and Intelligence Layers. The Knowledge Layer applies concepts of fuzzy sets theory to convey information from data sources, and the Intelligence Layer uses CI methods to create the routes considering the information obtained from the Knowledge Layer.

As a way of validating the FAR framework, a prototype was implemented, and simulations were performed. The details about this instantiation of the prototype were presented in Chap. 7. With the results obtained, the author dares to claim that better delivery routes can be obtained and thus a better performance of delivering parcels to customers.

The following section aligns the results and developments completed in this work with the research questions defined at the beginning of this book and discusses the findings.

8.2   Alignment with Research Questions and Discussion

This section is devoted to answering the research questions stated in Sect. 1.2, taking the outcome of the different artifacts implemented and the well-grounded academic research performed in the frame of this book.

RQ1: What are the main factors that affect the last-mile delivery efficiency?

With the literature review performed in Sect. 2.2, the participation of the author in a Makeathon, and workshops with Swiss Post, the issues that affect the last-mile delivery found in the literature were confirmed: most of the customers still prefer to get their packages delivered at home and they are not willing to share constantly their geographical location for the sake of receiving a parcel in time.

Furthermore, specifically in the case of Switzerland, alternatives such as leaving the package by a neighbor are no longer feasible as most people are constantly on the move and expect a now and everywhere type of service.

The conditions to attempt to improve the last mile are pretty restrictive. On the one hand, traffic has to be studied; companies that offer routing services such as Google are unwilling to provide their data to other businesses; others such as Here do not have enough coverage of cities. Thus, the geospatial data of the delivery vehicles have to be leveraged; even if they are not hundreds circulating, they still perform similar routes every day. On the other hand, suitable methods need to be found to approximate when a customer is at home and try to protect their privacy.

Even if the insights might not be as precise as desired, decisions can still be made when the data can be understood adequately and processed with adequate methods. Additionally, the new generation of information technology-powered services shall meet the requirements of all involved stakeholders' requirements while still being ethical and implemented with humanistic and sustainable principles.

RQ2: Which computational intelligence methods are suitable to obtain more efficient routes for the last-mile delivery?

Given that the data available to implement this work is uncertain, incomplete, and imprecise, suitable methods to address these issues to obtain insights and convey information had to be found.

Based on a state-of-the-art review and combined with an argumentative analysis, Chap. 3 illustrated how computational-based methods could be used under the restrictive conditions in which this research effort had to be developed. Two main CI theories were identified as helpful to achieve the goals of this project: fuzzy set theory and swarm intelligence.

Fuzzy set theory was presented as an extension of traditional sets with the difference that the elements can belong to more than one set to a certain degree for fuzzy sets. This property enabled to conduct an analysis and classification of traffic areas and customers' habits.

With linguistic summarizations, it was possible to understand traffic situations in a glimpse. They were a promising way of including a more comprehensive range of citizens in the development of Smart City, as information that seems complicated at first can be communicated with simple sentences.

On the other hand, swarm intelligence provided the guidelines to obtain delivery routes built upon the conditions of traffic and customers' presence at home. This agent-based modeling has the advantage of facilitating the understanding of how interactions in transportation are done, and with that, it was possible to discover the best way of visiting several locations while saving resources.

Even if those methods have been around for decades, they are often ignored as approaches that provide more precise results are on trend currently. The main reason for this could be the fact that even if human beings do not think in a binary manner, most computational systems work like that. For instance, companies have to meet service levels; even if the values are close to the acceptance levels for some indicator, they will be considered not achieved ultimately and thus the need to look for precise ways of meeting them. Moreover, for fuzzy and approximate methods to be more applied, better evaluation methods to guarantee the quality of the results they offer should be implemented.

RQ3: How to get insights about critical traffic areas in cities that potentially impact delivery routes?

As previously highlighted, with geospatial data of delivery trucks, it is possible to get insights into how traffic behaves. However, this data can be hard to aggregate to convey information.

An application that uses geospatial data and type-2 fuzzy sets were presented in Chap. 4. This artifact illustrated how segmenting the space with bounding boxes or geohashes is a convenient approach to analyze at different granular levels the speed and time that it takes to traverse those segments, at different times of the day. In this manner, data can be indexed and aggregated more easily.

Furthermore, by identifying variables of interest such as speed and travel time, it was illustrated how an indicator that depicts the traffic criticality in one area could be defined. Given that measuring and averaging speed and travel times can result in data with high variability, to capture and use such variability, type-2 fuzzy sets were used. Additionally, fuzzy rules and inference were used to score and identify the critical traffic areas.

Per the results of a case study applying the aforementioned process, it was found that this approach confirmed insights that the industry partners already had and also revealed new areas that were not suspected of presenting inconveniences to the circulation. However, one main limitation of the developed artifact is that it does not include real-time data, and thus, specific scores might not be representative of what is happening at a specific point in time. The author argues that having a reference about what typically happens when observing data over long periods of time still provides an approximate overview of the traffic conditions that can be used to adjust or create delivery route plans.

RQ4: How can postal customers be categorized without using explicit location data?

Provided that only data about the past deliveries were available, ways to categorize customers under this conditions needed to be established. To achieve such a goal, in Chap. 5, different classification methods were explored, from crisp clustering to a fuzzy inference system.

It was found that given the nature of the data, the fuzzy inference-based method was the most appropriate.

Modeling the behavior of a person with a dichotomy is far too complex, and thus, using the data of past deliveries and the K-means clustering did not offer good insights; its fuzzy variant was also not convenient given the available dataset. The outcome of the fuzzy rule-based method proved to provide better results, and thus this method was chosen as the means that enables such a classification.

Although humans usually exhibit habitual behavior, this is not the same every single day. Thus, with fuzzy methods, it was possible to capture such variability more appropriately to perform inferences. It was more useful to express *customer A is sometimes at home on Monday morning* than saying the customer *does not belong to the cluster of presence at home on Monday mornings*. Thus, fuzzy methods still granted the usage of data of such a nature to perform inferences, unlike crisp approaches.

However, one limitation of this method is that it is based on historical data. Therefore, when someone moves to a new place, no data will be available, and it would be impossible to approximate the presence of the person at home since most likely their habits have also changed.

RQ5: How can we reduce the first try delivery failure without compromising the customers' privacy?

With the studied theories, implementation of the artifacts for traffic analysis and customers' classification, argumentative-deductive analysis, and exchange with the industrial partners, it was possible to define the FAR conceptual framework in Chap. 7.

The FAR framework was defined to create delivery routes considering several aspects when choosing what is the best next location to visit. At its core, fuzzy methods are the means to obtain knowledge from the data, and the fuzzy ant system enables creating the routes.

The purpose of using this swarm intelligence approach was to take advantage that such method provides that a great part of the space of possibilities is explored since the task can be completed even if some of the agents fail, and the fact that the solution can be escalated and adapted given that the number of ants and nodes can be changed easily.

To validate that the first-try delivery failure can be reduced, an instantiation of the FAR framework was presented in Chap. 8. The traffic and customers' insights developed previously were leveraged by implementing fuzzy rules that enabled the agents of the fuzzy ant system to choose the best options of the next place to visit to create an improved version of a tour. With this method, the customers' privacy is not disrespected as the routes are created considering only the history of past deliveries and not an explicit location.

The experiments conducted and the comparisons with other well-established routing methods showed that the FAR prototype meets the goals of improving the first-try delivery tour while finding shorter routes that foster the saving of resources.

Despite the results obtained, the availability of real-time data remains an open issue. Sudden events such as the Covid-19 global pandemic directly influence the performance of this framework since it drastically changes the mobility on the streets and the presence of the people at home. However, the author argues that the FAR framework can still be used since fuzzy methods are applied to capture such variability and uncertainty; thus, with real-time data, the models can be adjusted and therefore still used. Nevertheless, tests under such conditions are still to be completed to verify that the results still meet the objectives.

8.3 Future Research

Considering the answers to the research questions and the analysis points on each of them, it was possible to define some direction for future research work.

By the current traffic data artifact development results, the principal focus of future development is to include real-time data to enhance the traffic criticality score. Naturally, the historical data are still helpful, but a model that balances the history and the current situation will be even closer to reality. Furthermore, aspects such as weather, events, and road works should be included in the inference model to adjust the scores faithfully.

Regarding the customers' categorization according to the past successful deliveries, problems such as when a new customer comes or changes direction should be addressed. This issue can be compared to the so-called cold start for recommender systems. Possible options could still be considering the history of the deliveries at the last place in a certain degree of the customer until new data are gathered. For a completely new customer, if the privacy wants to be preserved and no explicit information about preferred delivery times has to be asked, then the option will be to assign initially a state of *delivery sometimes successful* until new data are gathered and the classification updated.

Furthermore, as it was previously mentioned, the implementation of the FAR prototype is far from being a fully functional product. The current prototype has to be tested with more process-intensive tasks and the inclusion of real-time data. Moreover, more than adjusting the implementation functionality, this project's inclusion in developing a new product has to be studied. The adoption of the FAR prototype implies the development of a possible new business model. Thus, its effects on a company and the customers have to be carefully studied to succeed since it changes the traditional business model. Like any innovation, it entails risks and an investment of resources.

In addition, even if the traffic linguistic summaries artifact was not directly included in the current definition of the FAR framework, linguistic summarizations can still be included in the development of a project of this nature. It could be used, for instance, to inform the delivery personnel about the current or typical status of the traffic conditions. Another use case is to convey knowledge from feedback provided by the delivery personnel and the customers about the utility and effectiveness of the routes and deliveries. In this way, such feedback can be used to adjust the computation of the delivery tours.

To close the curtains in the future development and directions of the FAR conceptual framework, explainability aspects are yet to be included. Some first steps were performed by considering design constraints and guidelines for the computation of inferences, rules, and fuzzy sets for all the developed artifacts; nevertheless, having a fully explained system is yet to be achieved. In the current times, when our data are being used to train an infinity of systems and results are provided without most people having an idea of how they are obtained, explaining how such results are obtained is crucial toward more (digital) ethical Human-Smart Cities.

8.4   Outlook and Conclusions

Cities are moving to more sustainable development. Without a doubt, information technologies play an essential role in implementing solutions that foster such development. There is, however, a long way to go to achieve such goals.

Including people in the identification of problems and the conception of solutions is crucial. We are the managers of our present and future, and thus, it is rational to involve citizens in improving the places where we live, for us and the future generations. There is a current expansion of the usage of technologies and that has to be leveraged ethically. Nevertheless, the world is growing unequally, and such inequality is becoming broader.

Solutions attempting to improve the way we live in the cities should be developed in that direction. In this research work, a very punctual case was studied and developed. The results obtained might not be perceived as impactful to achieve the aforementioned in the short term. Nevertheless, some key aspects constitute the main contribution of this project:

- A way of developing solutions for logistics involving the know-how of people working in related industries, fostering the concept of collective intelligence
- An effective application of swarm intelligence algorithms for human-centered Smart City and logistic research
- A solution that aligns with the goals of improving mobility in the cities and thus a contribution to the implementation of Smart Cities is made
- The usage of uncertain, imprecise data to perform inferences and implement a fully working prototype for the identification of more convenient routes

The last point is to be highlighted since, nowadays, more attention is given to precise models that require large amounts of precise data (i.e., machine learning and neural network methods) and consume high amounts of energy. Thus, the author attempted to show how using soft computing techniques also enables practical solutions and not only theoretical ones as many developments in fuzzy logic.

Furthermore, Smart Mobility solutions should be conceived not only as a way of improving traffic per se but also as means to deliver information that enables redesigning networks and replanning routes. This endeavor attempts to achieve so, implying that a contribution is done to the key component of integrated information technology of the Smart City Wheel by Cohen (2015).

As for the FAR framework, the case presented in this book is only one example of its application. It was conceptualized to provide a computational intelligence-powered manner to visit different locations more efficiently under different conditions. The same concepts and methods could be applied to improve public transportation routing, navigation routes for drivers, and other areas of the supply chain deliveries such as connections between distribution points.

Looking further than the academic domain, the author believes a solution of this nature can potentially be developed into a start-up or a spin-off company. With an initial investment to purchase the required server infrastructure, a business plan, and the rights to use the data, it would not require too much time to implement the solution. It could start operating in the city of Bern (since the data used in this book come from that city) and later on implemented in other cities. It could be sold as a routing service through an interface to existing delivery companies in the first instance and move forward according to the results obtained.

References

Cohen, B. (2015). The smart city wheel. https://www.smart-circle.org/smartcity/blog/boyd-cohen-the-smart-city-wheel/. Accessed 04 Feb 2020.

Appendix A
Data Structures of Probe Data of Delivery Vehicles and Traffic Message Records Databases

Table A.1 Data structure of the probe data records ($DS_{1.1}$) used in the development of the FAR prototype

Field	Data type	Description
asset_name	String	Name of the vehicle
city	String	Name of the city where the vehicle is operating
driver_id	String	Identification of the driver
event_type	String	Type of event recorded (e.g., moving, parking, and breaking)
latitude	Float	Latitude of the position of the vehicle
location_id	Integer	Identification of the location of the vehicle
longitude	Float	Longitude of the position of the vehicle
mileage	Float	Mileage at the moment of recording
modul_id	Integer	Identification of the vehicle
position_time	Timestamp	Timestamp when the recording was performed
speed	Integer	Speed at the moment of recording
time_moved	Integer	Time that the vehicle was moving since the last recording
time_standing	Integer	Time that the vehicle was standing since the last recording
zip_code	String	ZIP code of the location where the vehicle is operating

© The Author(s), under exclusive license to Springer Nature Switzerland AG 2022
J. Pincay Nieves, *Smart Urban Logistics*, Fuzzy Management Methods,
https://doi.org/10.1007/978-3-031-16704-1

Table A.2 Data structure of the TMC records ($DS_{1.2}$) used in the development of the FAR prototype

Field	Data type	Description
nummer	Integer	Identification of the incident
strassennummer	String	Name of the road where the incident happened
start	String	Name of the location where the incident started
startcoordinatelat	Float	Latitude of the location where the incident started
startcoordinatelong	Float	Longitude of the location where the incident started
startlocationcode	Integer	Location code of the location where the incident started
end	String	Name of the location where the incident ended
endcoordinatelat	Float	Latitude of the location where the incident ended
endcoordinatelong	Float	Longitude of the location where the incident ended
endlocationcode	Integer	Location code of the location where the incident ended
richtung	String	Direction of the road in which the incident happened
kanton	String	Canton of Switzerland where the incident happened
startzeit	Timestamp	Timestamp when the incident started
endezeit	Timestamp	Timestamp when the incident ended
dauer	Interval	Duration of the incident
ereignisse	String	Description of the incident

Appendix B
Python Implementation of the Critical Traffic Areas Identification Artifact

Listing B.1 Python implementation of the type-2 fuzzy sets for travel time (tt), segmented speed (ss), traffic criticality (tc), and the fuzzy rules used for inference

```
1
2 #Definition of the domain and sets of the input variable travel
      time (tt)
3 domain1 = linspace(0.02, 2, 50000)
4 short = IT2FS_Gaussian_UncertMean(domain1, [0.02, 0.1, 0.15, 1.])
5 medium = IT2FS_Gaussian_UncertMean(domain1,
6                                    [0.59, 0.1, 0.15, 1.])
7 long = IT2FS_Gaussian_UncertMean(domain1, [1.2, 0.1, 0.15, 1.])
8 very_long = IT2FS_Gaussian_UncertMean(domain1,
9                                       [2.0, 0.1, 0.2, 1.])
10
11 #Definition of the domain and sets of the input variable segment
       speed (ss)
12 domain2 = linspace(0.0, 1.2, 50000)
13 very_low = IT2FS_Gaussian_UncertMean(domain2, [0.0, 0.08, 0.09,
       1.])
14 low = IT2FS_Gaussian_UncertMean(domain2, [0.40, 0.08, 0.09, 1.])
15 normal = IT2FS_Gaussian_UncertMean(domain2,
16                                    [0.80, 0.08, 0.09, 1.])
17 high = IT2FS_Gaussian_UncertMean(domain2, [1.2, 0.08, 0.07, 1.])
18
19 #Definition of the domain and sets of the output variable traffic
       criticality (tc)
20 domain3 = linspace(0.0, 1, 50000)
21 not_critical = IT2FS_Gaussian_UncertMean(domain3,
22                                          [0.0, 0.07, 0.07, 1.])
23 low_critical = IT2FS_Gaussian_UncertMean(domain3,
24                                          [0.35, 0.07, 0.07, 1.])
25 critical = IT2FS_Gaussian_UncertMean(domain3,
26                                      [0.7, 0.07, 0.07, 1.])
27 highly_critical = IT2FS_Gaussian_UncertMean(domain3,
28                                             [1.0, 0.07, 0.07, 1.])
```

© The Author(s), under exclusive license to Springer Nature Switzerland AG 2022
J. Pincay Nieves, *Smart Urban Logistics*, Fuzzy Management Methods,
https://doi.org/10.1007/978-3-031-16704-1

```
29
30  #Definition of the Mamdani fuzzy inference system
31  myIT2FLS = Mamdani(min_t_norm, max_s_norm)
32  myIT2FLS.add_input_variable("tt")
33  myIT2FLS.add_input_variable("ss")
34  myIT2FLS.add_output_variable("tc")
35
36  #Fuzzy rules of the inference system
37  myIT2FLS.add_rule([("tt", short), ("ss", high)],
38                    [("tc", not_critical)])
39  myIT2FLS.add_rule([("tt", short), ("ss", normal)],
40                    [("tc", not_critical)])
41  myIT2FLS.add_rule([("tt", short), ("ss", low)],
42                    [("tc", low_critical)])
43  myIT2FLS.add_rule([("tt", short), ("ss", very_low)],
44                    [("tc", critical)])
45  myIT2FLS.add_rule([("tt", medium), ("ss", high)],
46                    [("tc", low_critical)])
47  myIT2FLS.add_rule([("tt", medium), ("ss", normal)],
48                    [("tc", low_critical)])
49  myIT2FLS.add_rule([("tt", medium), ("ss", low)],
50                    [("tc", critical)])
51  myIT2FLS.add_rule([("tt", medium), ("ss", very_low)],
52                    [("tc", critical)])
53  myIT2FLS.add_rule([("tt", long), ("ss", high)],
54                    [("tc", critical)])
55  myIT2FLS.add_rule([("tt", long), ("ss", normal)],
56                    [("tc", critical)])
57  myIT2FLS.add_rule([("tt", long), ("ss", low)],
58                    [("tc", highly_critical)])
59  myIT2FLS.add_rule([("tt", long), ("ss", very_low)],
60                    [("tc", highly_critical)])
61  myIT2FLS.add_rule([("tt", very_long), ("ss", high)],
62                    [("tc", critical)])
63  myIT2FLS.add_rule([("tt", very_long), ("ss", normal)],
64                    [("tc", critical)])
65  myIT2FLS.add_rule([("tt", very_long), ("ss", low)],
66                    [("tc", highly_critical)])
67  myIT2FLS.add_rule([("tt", very_long), ("ss", very_low)],
68                    [("tc", highly_critical)])
```

Appendix C
Sample of Fuzzy Rules for the Customers' Presence at Home During the Mornings

Listing C.1 Python implementation of the fuzzy rules to approximate the customers' presence at home during the mornings

```
 1
 2 #all always -> always
 3 R1="IF (MondayMorning IS always) AND (TuesdayMorning IS always)
 4 AND (WednesdayMorning IS always) AND (ThursdayMorning IS always)
 5 AND (FridayMorning IS always)
 6 THEN (Morning IS always)"
 7
 8 #four always + one mostly -> always
 9 R2="IF (MondayMorning IS mostly) AND (TuesdayMorning IS always)
10 AND (WednesdayMorning IS always) AND (ThursdayMorning IS always)
11 AND (FridayMorning IS always)
12 THEN (Morning IS always)"
13
14 #two always + three mostly -> mostly
15 R17="IF (MondayMorning IS always) AND (TuesdayMorning IS always)
16 AND (WednesdayMorning IS mostly) AND (ThursdayMorning IS mostly)
17 AND (FridayMorning IS mostly)
18 THEN (Morning IS mostly)"
19
20 #one always + four mostly -> mostly
21 R27="IF (MondayMorning IS always) AND (TuesdayMorning IS mostly)
22 AND (WednesdayMorning IS mostly) AND (ThursdayMorning IS mostly)
23 AND (FridayMorning IS mostly)
24 THEN (Morning IS mostly)"
25
26 #two always + three rarely -> sometimes
27 R47="IF (MondayMorning IS always) AND (TuesdayMorning IS always)
28 AND (WednesdayMorning IS rarely) AND (ThursdayMorning IS rarely)
29 AND (FridayMorning IS rarely)
30 THEN (Morning IS sometimes)"
31
32 #two mostly + three rarely -> sometimes
```

```
33  R108="IF (MondayMorning IS mostly) AND (TuesdayMorning IS mostly)
34  AND (WednesdayMorning IS rarely) AND (ThursdayMorning IS rarely)
35  AND (FridayMorning IS rarely)
36  THEN (Morning IS sometimes)"
37
38  # one mostly + four rarely -> rarely
39  R118="IF (MondayMorning IS mostly) AND (TuesdayMorning IS rarely)
40  AND (WednesdayMorning IS rarely) AND (ThursdayMorning IS rarely)
41  AND (FridayMorning IS rarely)
42  THEN (Morning IS rarely)"
43
44  # three never + two rarely -> never
45  R169="IF (MondayMorning IS rarely) AND (TuesdayMorning IS rarely)
46  AND (WednesdayMorning IS never) AND (ThursdayMorning IS never)
47  AND (FridayMorning IS never)
48  THEN (Morning IS never)"
49
50  # two always + two rarely + one never -> sometimes
51  R605 = "IF (MondayMorning IS always) AND (TuesdayMorning IS
        always)
52  AND (WednesdayMorning IS rarely) AND (ThursdayMorning IS rarely)
53  AND (FridayMorning IS never)
54  THEN (Morning IS sometimes)"
55
56  # two mostly + two rarely + one always -> mostly
57  R695 = "IF (MondayMorning IS rarely) AND (TuesdayMorning IS
        rarely)
58  AND (WednesdayMorning IS mostly) AND (ThursdayMorning IS mostly)
59  AND (FridayMorning IS always)
60  THEN (Morning IS mostly)"
61
62  # two mostly + two never + one always -> sometimes
63  R725 = "IF (MondayMorning IS never) AND (TuesdayMorning IS never)
64  AND (WednesdayMorning IS mostly) AND (ThursdayMorning IS mostly)
65  AND (FridayMorning IS always)
66  THEN (Morning IS sometimes)"
```

Appendix D
Python Implementation of the FAS Algorithm

Listing D.1 Python implementation of the FAS algorithm utility to move to the next node

```
def move_ants(space, locations_df,  positions, distance,
     pheromones, fas_parameters):
    """This function moves the ants among the nodes of the space
       to find the best locations

    Arguments:
        space:  Sample space
        locations_df: Locations to visit
        starting_positions: Initial location of the antes
        distance: Distance between the nodes
        pheromones:  Amount of pheromones at each link
        fas_parameters: alpha, beta, tau parameters

    Returns:
        numpy.ndarray: Path taken by the ant
    """
    #Definition of the fuzzy system
    FS=defineFuzzySystem()

    paths = np.zeros((space.shape[0],
            positions.shape[0]),
            dtype=int) - 1
    next_location_utility = np.zeros((space.shape[0]),
                        dtype=float)
    paths[0]  = positions

    #Iterate over all nodes
    for node in range(1, space.shape[0]):
        for ant in range(positions.shape[0]):
            #Computation of the utility to go to the next node
            for i in range(1, space.shape[0]):
                distance=distance[positions[ant]][i]
```

```
33              pheromones_val= pheromones[positions[ant]][i]
34              delivery_success= locations_df.iloc[i]
35                             ["Monday_morning"]
36              traffic_score=locations_df.iloc[i]
37                                     ["TRAFFICSCORE"]
38
39              FS.set_variable('Distance', distance)
40              FS.set_variable('PheromoneIntensity',
41                             pheromones_val)
42              FS.set_variable('DeliverySuccess',
43                             delivery_success)
44              FS.set_variable('TrafficCriticality',
45                              traffic_score)
46              next_location_utility[i]=FS.Sugeno_inference(
47                             ["Utility"],
48                             verbose=True)['Utility']
49          # Index to maximum probability node
50          next_pos = np.argwhere(next_location_utility == np.
        amax(next_location_utility))[0][0]
51
52          while next_pos in paths[:, ant]:
53              next_location_utility[next_pos] = 0.0
54              next_pos = np.argwhere(
55              next_location_utility ==
56              np.amax(next_location_utility))[0][0]
57          paths[node, ant] = next_pos
58          #Update pheromones
59          pheromones[node, next_pos] =
60                                 pheromones[node, next_pos] +
61                                 fas_parameters[2]
62      return np.swapaxes(paths, 0, 1)
```

Acronyms

ACO   Ant Colony Optimization. xix, xxi, xxiii, 45, 47, 48, 49, 50, 51, 122, 139, 144, 145

AI   Artificial Intelligence. 47

B2C   Business to Consumer. 89, 90

CI   Computational Intelligence. 4, 5, 26, 45, 52, 107, 152, 153

FAR   Fuzzy Ant Routing. xviii, xix, xxi, xxii, xxiii, 10, 113, 114, 115, 116, 117, 118, 120, 121, 122, 125, 126, 127, 128, 129, 134, 135, 136, 137, 138, 139, 141, 143, 144, 145, 146, 152, 155, 156, 157

FAS   Fuzzy Ant System. xv, xix, xxi, xxiii, 45, 46, 49, 50, 116, 117, 118, 120, 121, 122, 126, 131, 132, 133, 134, 135, 137, 139, 141, 165

FOU   Footprint of Uncertainty. 37, 74

GDPR   General Data Protection Regulation. 22, 89

GPS   Global Positioning Systems. 4, 25, 60, 65, 77

IFC   Inductive Fuzzy Classification. 90

IT2 FLS   Interval Type-2 Fuzzy Logic System. xviii, xxi, 61, 67, 69, 70, 71, 72

IT2 FS   Interval Type-2 Fuzzy Sets. xviii, 37, 60, 61, 69, 70, 77

LS   Linguistic Summary. xviii, xxi, 74, 76, 77, 78, 80, 81, 84

PCA   Principal Component Analysis. 93, 95, 96, 98, 101

RFM   Recency, Frequency, Monetary Value. 90

T2 FS   Type-2 Fuzzy Sets. 36, 37, 60, 61, 74

TCP   Traveling Salesman Problem. 46, 48

TMC   Traffic Message Channel. 65, 72, 76, 77, 84, 85

VRP   Vehicle Routing Problem. 25, 26, 50

© The Author(s), under exclusive license to Springer Nature Switzerland AG 2022   167
J. Pincay Nieves, *Smart Urban Logistics*, Fuzzy Management Methods,
https://doi.org/10.1007/978-3-031-16704-1

Glossary

Collective Intelligence   Collective intelligence refers to a network of individual intelligence, such as people and/or objects, that are more efficient together than individually by themselves. 8

Design Science Research   Design science research investigates the design of innovative artifacts to solve real-world problems. In information systems, such artifacts can be constructs, models, methods, and social innovations relating to information and communication technologies. 6

Fuzzy Inference System   They are computing frameworks that enable reaching a conclusion applying concepts of fuzzy sets, linguistic variables, and fuzzy rules. They are also known as fuzzy logic controllers, or fuzzy expert systems. 41

Fuzzy Rules   Fuzzy rules are the bridge that enables the forming of knowledge from individual pieces of imprecise information. They are more flexible IF-THEN rules. 33

Geohash   Geohash (or geohashing) is one example of a geospatial index. Geohash is a hierarchical spatial data structure based on the Z-order curve. A Z-order curve is a space-filling curve that iterates through space in a Z manner. Geohashing iteratively subdivides space into grid buckets or bounding boxes, producing different precision at various hierarchies. 61

Linguistic Variable   They are variables whose values are words expressed in natural language and are primarily combinations of adverbs (e.g., most of, some, and always) and adjectives (e.g., critical, warm, and tall). Linguistic variables are possible thanks to the concepts behind fuzzy sets and membership functions. 33

Smart Logistics   Improvement of mobility aspects of a city when they are not related to public transportation but to logistics and delivery services. 3

J. Pincay Nieves, *Smart Urban Logistics*, Fuzzy Management Methods,
https://doi.org/10.1007/978-3-031-16704-1

Smart City   The enrichment of city functions through the use of information technologies with the goal of developing sustainable and citizen-friendly services. The collection and usage of city data is an important aspect that Smart Cities handle toward building more liveable and viable spaces. 3

Transdisciplinary Research   Transdisciplinary research is a collaboration of researchers from different disciplines and practice partners from different companies and institutions working jointly. They exchange information, share resources, and integrate disciplines to achieve a common scientific and practice relevant goal. 6

Printed in the United States
by Baker & Taylor Publisher Services